Maintenance Man to Millionaire

Real Estate Wealth Creation for Everyday People

Glenn C. Gonzales

Maintenance Man to Millionaire
Real Estate Wealth Creation for Everyday People

Printed by B.C. Allen Publishing and Tonic Books
144 N 7th St. #525
Brooklyn, NY 11249

Now taking manuscript submissions and book ideas at any stage of the process:
submissions@tonicbooks.online

Printed in the United States of America

Cover Design: Zeeshan Haque
Interior Design: Susan Veach
Editor: Krista Munster
Production: Jade Maniscalco

ISBN: 978-1-950977-95-6

DEDICATION

This book is dedicated to my loving and supportive wife, Heidi Gonzales. She has been a tremendous inspiration. She fought for her life and showed me what it means to be brave and strong despite all obstacles.

I also dedicate this book to my posterity, that they might learn and grow from my experiences. I pray that this book be an inspiration and an insight to what we have gone through as a family. May the Lord bless our future generations.

To all the individuals who have been a part of my experiences along the way, you have been my mentors, guides, and friends through all the ups and downs. You have been my bosses, employees, and peers. Thank you for helping me along the way.

And to each of you striving to improve and inspire yourself and those around you, you are making a difference!

TABLE OF CONTENTS

FOREWORD:

THE RAGS-TO-RICHES PATH

BY ROD KHLEIF

Before Glenn Gonzales agreed to be interviewed on my *The Lifetime Cash Flow Through Real Estate Investing Podcast,* we'd never met. I knew him only by his impressive reputation. Glenn is hugely successful, and he has earned a lot of respect from his peers in the real estate industry.

Yet, as we talked about his early days in property management and how that led to founding his own multifamily firm, the man I discovered was humble, humorous, and generous. He impressed me with his sincere wish to give back and add value so that others might benefit from his knowledge. That's why I invited him to participate in a mastermind meeting I was hosting at my home, where we became fast friends.

Maybe I was drawn to Glenn's temperament and personality because I have lived my own rags-to-riches story. As a young, impoverished Dutch immigrant, I struggled to support my family. Nice clothes, plentiful food, and all the other earmarks of a stable economic foundation were beyond our reach. But I had a burning desire to find my way and do better.

Like Glenn, I've had remarkable triumphs and spectacular failures. Some people call that type of cycle the School of Hard Knocks. I gratefully refer to those events as the "seminars" that taught me so much about life and building enduring wealth.

What you hold in your hand is not just a book. It is Glenn's personal and, at times, harrowing story. And it is his gift to you. His journey from maintenance man to millionaire is proof that nothing is out of reach for the man or woman who is willing to learn and take some leaps of faith. I believe his remarkable path will move your heart and inspire you to reconsider what is within your grasp.

Maintenance Man to Millionaire: Real Estate Wealth Creation for Everyday People is for anyone that knows they deserve more from life but don't know how to achieve it. The book gives practical, first-hand knowledge and tips to anyone wanting to learn how to invest in multifamily real estate.

Yet the remarkable thing about Glenn's book is that it resonates not only for beginners, but for seasoned operators like me. There are so many great takeaways in these pages that even I was jotting notes. After all, the many nuances included herein can come only from a seasoned professional like Glenn Gonzales.

I got a lot of value from Glenn's ideas about leadership. To build a business the size and scope of his multimillion-dollar asset management firm requires a savvy, expert leader who has an appreciation for people and their natural gifts. Glenn is not only wealthy; he is resourceful and shares some simple but keen strategies that anyone can begin to practice, no matter what type of work they do.

I give this book my highest recommendation and believe you will enjoy it as much as this rags-to-riches kid did.

Rod Khleif
Entrepreneur and author of *The Multifamily Property Toolbook*

ONE
———

THE VALUE OF YOU

Value was on my mind when I sat with one of my property managers and began teaching him some real estate calculations. The information was new to him, so he struggled with it at first. But the longer we sat at his desk at the property, it became clear that it wasn't the numbers that bewildered him. Finally, he said it out loud.

"Why are you teaching me all this?" he asked. "I'm just the property manager. I don't own the building. You do."

He was right. My company had taken possession of the multifamily apartment building because our analysis told us it would make us money if, for starters, we improved each unit and upgraded the curb appeal. And that's exactly what had happened. But we could not have improved the value of that property without the manager's help and knowledge.

I answered with a question of my own.

"How do you know you're doing a good job?"

"You haven't fired me?" he said.

I laughed. He had a point. Doing good work is an excellent way of assuring employment. And, in some ways, that is a measure of value that he can take pride in. But I wasn't satisfied. I wanted him to expand his appreciation for what he was contributing and accomplishing.

"Okay, we agree. Nobody around here wants to fire you because you've made a difference. You've helped us succeed. But how can you know that beyond a shadow of a doubt?" I said.

I didn't wait for the answer I knew he couldn't provide. Instead, I jotted some figures on my legal pad and then reached for a calculator and worked some numbers, and soon, I had a large figure.

"This was the value of the apartment complex when we bought it a year or so ago," I said.

He was impressed. "Woohoo. That's a lot."

"Yeah. That's a lot of money, right? Now, let's go back to the formula we were working on. What's the first term I gave you?"

"Annual net operating income."

"NOI. Right. And we divide that by—"

"The cap rate," he said.

"Yeah, the rate of capitalization. We divide annual NOI by the cap rate, and we get what?"

"The value of the property," he answered.

He was a good learner and a smart man. He understood the math. Now, I was going to blow his mind with an even more important lesson.

I cleared the calculator and encouraged him to watch the screen as I started punching in a new set of figures. When I finished, I asked, "How do you like them apples?"

He stared at the calculator, not sure how to answer. "What does it mean?"

The number I showed him was the new, improved value of the property he managed. He was shocked.

"Wow. You added that much value in a year?" he asked.

"Not me. *You.*"

"Me? What are you talking about? I'm not the—"

I said, "I know you're not the owner. I'm the owner."

We both laughed. Then I went on to explain.

When our bid for the building was successful, we knew we could add value by raising the rent by about $80 per apartment. If you have 350 apartments, for example, that money adds up. Tenants and new folks looking for a nice place to live will pay a little more if they see improvements, and they know they can get quick responses from management when a faucet doesn't work, or the heating unit is on the blink.

"You manage this property well. Tenants don't wait long for maintenance, the grounds always look great, and each day, you stayed disciplined and focused. You help make this a wonderful place to live."

This humble man was speechless for a moment, but his face lit up with pride.

"Let's go back to my original question: how do you know you're doing a good job?"

"Get out the calculator?" he asked.

"Exactly. You crunch the numbers. And then what do you do?"

His face went blank, like a kid who can't answer the teacher's question at school.

"You negotiate a raise."

Now he was truly baffled. He shook his head and looked at me like I'd gone nuts. I'm the owner of the building, his boss, and I'm telling him he should ask me for more money.

"What? Wow. Glenn, nobody has ever taken the time to teach me this. You're the only one who explains why I do what I do. But you'll lose money if I ask for a raise, won't you?"

"Not *ask*," I said. "Negotiate, based on facts."

He nodded, smiling, another lesson learned. "Okay, I get it. But why are you telling me all this?"

"Because I value what you do for us. I value who you are. And your life will get better and better when *you* can put a value on what you bring to the table."

The Cold Truth

The difference between a maintenance man and a millionaire is knowledge. It's not luck or rich parents or the kind of car you drive. Money is what we all want because we know our quality of life improves when we're not worried about paying the bills. But knowledge is the match that lights the flame of wellbeing and fulfillment.

My introduction to real estate happened way back when I was in college in Utah. At the time, my wife was an apartment leasing consultant, and I was asked if I would help with maintenance at the complex.

It was a good job. I painted apartments, fixed toilets, and other similar tasks. I also picked up the trash, which demanded that I spend time outside, and it was frigidly cold out. One day, while I was shivering, I started thinking that I'd much rather be inside leasing apartments or answering the phone.

I went to the regional manager of the real estate firm that managed the multifamily complex and said, "Hey, I think I'd rather be a manager."

She looked me up and down and finally said, "You're kidding, right?"

No. I wasn't kidding. "I think I could do that."

"Uh-huh. Well, I'll keep you in mind."

It wasn't exactly a ringing, singing endorsement. Maybe she didn't immediately warm to the idea because my work as a maintenance guy wasn't that good.

But a couple of months later, she called and said, "I don't know if you're going to like this, but I've got a small 60-unit apartment complex where we could use you to manage part-time and do maintenance part-time. What do you think?"

I'm like, *right on*. It felt like I'd hit a home run. I didn't know how to play it cool or say that I'd think it over. I jumped at the chance. "I'll take it. I'll take it."

It's obvious now what the regional manager was doing, right? It was a two-for-the-price-of-one kind of thing. The company couldn't afford both a full-time maintenance guy and a full-time manager because the building was so small. Sixty units is nothing—peanuts. But so what? The experience was my reward. And it made me feel great telling people I managed an apartment complex. Yeah, me, a college kid. I was now *management*.

I was good at leasing. I liked people, and it was a kick to help them find a nice place to live. The new tenants all seemed to like me, too—until they figured out that I was not great at maintenance. Here's how it would go.

The apartments I leased were pretty nice places— Shadow Mountain Townhomes. I'd rent a unit and give the folks a renters' move-in check-list. If something in their townhome was not working properly, they'd check it off and bring the list to my office. It was a simple concept—sort of.

During the day, while the tenants were at work, I'd go to their homes and fix whatever was on the list. Perfect. They'd never know that the manager of the place was also Mr. Fix-it. But then, the complaints started rolling in.

Late one day, a guy came to my office and complained, "Man, I don't know who fixed my apartment, but everything is still not working right."

Busted. I was so embarrassed. To cover myself, I'd say, "Darn. Sorry. I'll take care of it."

You see, he didn't know yet that I played a dual role, right? So, the next day, I'd grab my toolbox and return to the scene of the crime and, sure enough, I'd realize that I hadn't checked the dishwasher, or one of the burners on the electric stove wasn't heating up. Unfortunately, the guy who filed the complaint came home before I could finish my handy work.

"Hey, what are you doing here?" he asked.

Busted again. A full confession followed.

"Well, I am the manager, but I'm also the maintenance guy."

That was the end of the romance. It was terribly awkward for the resident to realize that the leasing guy he liked so much was a fake fixer-upper. And it was awkward for me to realize that I sucked at maintenance.

Do you realize now why I have so much respect for the people who manage or do maintenance on my properties? A manager cannot succeed without a skilled maintenance person. Neither fully succeeds without understanding the value they bring.

My entry-level job led to other opportunities. Eventually, I became the manager of large complexes that required a good deal of planning and maintenance. I always felt good when my employers, the owners of those properties, sold an asset for a profit. I knew I'd done my job well. There was a problem, though, that frankly, I had not considered until my wife Heidi fatefully and gently jabbed an elbow into my ribs.

"You're making a lot of people a lot of money. Why don't you do it yourself?"

Backward Progress

The good people I know often don't give themselves much credit. This was true of the manager I mentioned earlier who quickly grasped the formula for determining value: NOI divided by the cap rate. By learning one trick of the trade, he expanded his self-esteem.

After my wife nudged me to think bigger, I was forced to do a personal assessment. By then, I'd clocked about 25 years in the world of real estate. I was making a decent living and enjoyed praise for the work I did, but I owned no equity in the properties that were selling for millions of dollars.

In short, throughout the years, property management had taught me more than I realized. In some ways, I took my education for granted. I liked my work but unconsciously reduced its value by thinking of it only as a job, a career, not necessarily a profound store of knowledge that was valuable to others. I hadn't properly assessed how much I'd gained.

By the time I'd finished looking back, I had convinced myself that it was time to move forward and be an owner, not just an employee. Yes, I had a lot of experience and was respected in my field. But there was another more important element that was obvious from the time I took that first manager-maintenance job. I enjoyed people and had developed great relationships within my industry. Men and women trusted me for my work ethic and honesty. When you think about it, that's a pot of gold. All I had to do was find a way to put that value in the bank.

Eventually, I did. And I earned my first million dollars.

Sometimes, I wake up in the morning, and I have to pinch myself because I love where I'm at, and I love what I'm doing.

But it's been a journey, for sure. I've taken some hits, survived, and then thrived in ways I didn't think possible until I'd done a self-assessment.

My children tease me about my way of repeating life lessons as though they are proverbs. They call them *Glennisms*. As we move forward and I reveal how you, too, can improve your financial and personal life (two sides of the same coin), I'm going to share a few.

GLENNISM #1:

TO MOVE FORWARD, YOU MUST LOOK BACK

Assess your past. Jot down each job you've held and the lessons you learned. Also, recall the relationships that have taught you something, for better or worse. List your tangible skills (like carpentry or auto mechanics) and intangible skills (like emotional stability, kindness, zest for life). Begin to see your past as a store of knowledge and, therefore, value. Give yourself some credit for what you have already achieved.

NOTES AND THOUGHTS

_____

_____

_____

_____

_____

_____

_____

_____

TWO

THE BIG TRANSITION

There is one sure way to make progress in your real estate career: Do good work. As you already know, I was a lousy maintenance man. That type of job would never be my path to success.

But it might be yours. If maintenance is your day job, always do your best. Do your tasks so well that people notice. Remember, where you are now is not necessarily where you will be in a few months or a year. Your career will evolve in a way that is unique to you. So even if you crave change and advancement and maybe feel some frustration, do not doubt the importance of being dependable now in whatever work you do. Dependability is a stepping stone to better things.

I learned this a year after accepting the dual role of manager and maintenance man at the Shadow Mountain Townhomes. By then, all 60 units were occupied, and therefore, the cash flow of the asset had improved. That was important because now the owners could put more money into the complex, which improved its curb appeal.

My boss was impressed with what I had accomplished.

"Glenn, you've stabilized the performance of that building. No other manager was able to do that for us," she said.

That news excited me. Maybe full occupancy at Shadow Mountain would lead me up the ladder to regional manager. I was eager for a promotion. But my boss had another idea.

"Glenn, we've got a 200-unit building that is not doing well. We want you to look at it and share some ideas with the manager. You worked your magic at Shadow Mountain. Now, let's see if you can make it happen again," she said.

I took the bait because helping manage two separate properties allowed me to use the title *area* manager. It was another step up.

The larger complex was mostly applying the principles of success. Each unit looked nice, and they were correctly priced to be competitive in the given market. So why was this place underperforming?

There are three principles in commercial real estate that I'd learned from one guru or another. I've done so much reading on the topic that, frankly, I don't recall who put it so simply. My apologies for not naming names. But this concept is worth considering:

Product—Price—People

Two of the three P's were right on. But the third ...

My boss praised my success and believed it was the result of learning the real estate business from the ground up. I'd gotten my hands dirty as a maintenance guy and all that. But she was not entirely correct in her analysis of my skills.

When I showed Shadow Mountain to apartment hunters, I was not just a tour guide. I stepped beyond the "manager" job description and behaved like an enthusiastic friend. I helped each visitor imagine how it would feel to live there. I pointed out the benefits and compared my site to other buildings nearby. Yes, I had some sales savvy in my bones, and I was not afraid to express myself.

That's why I quickly spotted the reason the 200-unit complex was not fully occupied. I pulled the manager into a private conversation.

"You have great apartments. The price is right. But, I'm not trying to hurt anybody's feelings, okay? Your leasing agent has no personality," I said as diplomatically as I could.

Product. Price. *People.*

Right?

Does my criticism sound superficial? It's not. A sales-person doesn't need to flash a big, bright smile all the time. There is no need to be "fake" or pushy. But he or she does have to create a positive experience for the buyer, a personal connection. Unfortunately, apartment hunters who visited the complex were not wowed or charmed after their time with the leasing agent.

The manager of the building resisted my insight. She didn't want to fire the employee whom she considered a friend. I knew I would not be able to convince her that I was right, so I used another strategy.

"Look, you don't have to take my word for it. Let's bring in a *secret shopper* who can give you a second opinion."

It's common practice in all kinds of businesses. You want to know what impact your sales team is having, right? This is true in retail, banking, and real estate. The spying is a way of restoring objectivity, which the manager had lost.

Sure enough, our secret shopper reported that it was difficult to connect with the leasing agent. It was not her job to suggest we replace the employee. But the evaluation certainly implied what we must do next.

Even with two identical opinions, the manager struggled with what she had to do next. It's hard to fire someone knowing you are taking away their income. On the other hand, her lack of objectivity deepened the problem. Not only was the leasing agent hurting business, but the manager was too close to the situation to accept an obvious solution. And as a result, she was harming her own career. If your management style is not helping investors make money, how long do you think you'll have that job?

Thankfully, the manager finally saw the light and made the change. In time, that 200-unit property's occupancy and cash flow improved.

Simple, simple. Did it take a rocket scientist or mathematician to figure it out? Did you need ten years of real estate experience to solve the riddle?

Of course not, and that's the lesson to be learned about advancing your career in real estate: Do not underestimate the skills you already have, such as a friendly personality, an engaging temperament, and common sense. But most important is a willingness to learn. After all, the Shadow Mountain folks weren't just putting more money into their property after achieving higher occupancy. In a sense, they were investing in me, the guy who had improved their cash flow.

The same will be true for you if you use your skills as a painter, electrician, etc. to provide value. Invest in who you are, in your confidence to deliver, and doors will begin to open for you.

Fit the Job to the Person

To some degree, my heart went out to the manager as she faced the personnel decision. When we make an employment change, we fear we may have created pain for someone. But did we? The truth is, we may have done that person a favor.

If you are not good at leasing apartments, what good will it do you to stay in that job? Find work that suits your personality and aspirations. Constant failure is what causes the real pain. Move on.

I had this problem at about the same time I was moving up the real estate management ladder. My college days were coming to an end. As I completed a degree in behavioral science and health, I got an administrative internship at a hospital. Oh boy, lucky me. Finally, I was out of the classroom and into the real world, a world I quickly learned I hated.

Has it happened to you? Four college years flash by (in my case, it took six years to earn the degree because I had to keep a job while going to school). You do the work, get good grades, and can't wait for graduation day so that your professional life can begin. You'll have a nice home, a great car, a family. Your dreams are so vivid you can almost reach out and touch them. Then, you stub your toe and bump up against a terrible truth: you chose the wrong career.

I'm not the first guy who came to this realization. I know a former Navy man, for example, who worked hard to become an emergency room doctor—only to realize he might never survive his career choice. It was not that he lacked talent and smarts. He just knew that a couple of decades in that stressful environment would ruin him and his family. He is now the cofounder of a real estate syndication firm and loving life.

We sometimes push ourselves into things because we think it is practical, safe, expected of us, or impressive to others. Those considerations are fine unless you discover your heart shrinking because you are miserable in your career.

Fortunately, I was enjoying my work as a property manager. I'd helped improve a couple of buildings, and that fed a hunger in me to advance in real estate. After suffering through a boring hospital administration internship, I decided to sit down with my boss and lay it all on the line.

"Administrative stuff, pushing paper is not for me. I want property management to be my career. I'm serious about it. I'm ready for more challenges. How can I move up?" I asked.

Remember the first time I told her I was tired of maintenance and wanted to move into management? She was skeptical. But this meeting was different. Once we hired a new leasing agent at the 200-unit site, the closing ratio improved, as did occupancy and cash flow. She knew I was good at my job. I'd worked my magic right before her eyes.

"If you really want this, your next step is earning your CPM™ designation," she said.

"What is that?"

She explained that CPM stands for Certified Property Management, a designation I would have to earn from the Institute of Real Estate Management.

I was ready to roll. "Okay. How long will it take?"

"Well, that depends."

Becoming a Certified Property Manager is a big step and a mark of distinction. Investors require it so that they know their properties are being managed by capable hands.

I'd finished the fun and grind of college and hadn't expected to go after what would amount to another degree in a new profession. And I must admit, when I looked over the CPM requirements, I felt overwhelmed and intimidated. Oh man, I thought, this is big. This is bigger than me. This is for people in the profession. Then I realized, hey, wait a minute, *I* am in the profession. But there were roadblocks.

The cost of the training was more than I could afford. Heck, I'd just finished college.

Huge chunks of time for testing were also required, and that would require me to take unpaid leaves of absence from my job. The list below, provided by the Institute of Real Estate Management, is similar to what I stared at all those years ago:

- Three years (36 months) of qualifying real estate management experience as defined by IREM (portfolio and function minimums)

COMPLETE SEVEN REQUIRED COURSES.
Recommended order:

- Budgeting, Cash Flow, and Reporting for Investment Real Estate
- Marketing and Leasing Strategies for Retail Properties
- Or Marketing and Leasing Strategies for Multifamily Properties
- Or Marketing and Leasing Strategies for Office Buildings
- Leading a Winning Property Management Team
- Managing Maintenance Operations and Property Risk
- Financing and Loan Analysis for Investment Real Estate
- Performance and Valuation of Investment Real Estate

- Asset Analysis of Investment Real Estate
- Pass the CPM Certification exam
- Pass management plan on an actual property
- Attend Ethics for the Real Estate Manager and pass exam
- Pledge to uphold the IREM Code of Professional Ethics
- Acquire three professional reference letters
- Fulfill the one-year candidacy period by being a CPM Candidate Member, ARM Member, or ACoM Member in good standing for the 12 months prior to CPM approval
- Be in good standing with annual national and chapter dues
- Submit a CPM application with the application fee, which is $210
- Be current with annual national and chapter dues
- Hold a real estate license or verify that you are not required to have one for your current position
- Be affiliated with the NATIONAL ASSOCIATION OF REALTORS®
- Attend two IREM Chapter meetings or events during the 12 months immediately prior to CPM approval

- Be approved by your IREM Chapter

Do you see why the whole thing hit me like a ton of building bricks? I was reeling from the enormous challenge of moving forward in my career.

Yet, the coursework would teach me tenant managing strategies and investment property maintenance. I also had to learn the laws that rule the rights of renters, as well as property owners. The study would require a deep dive into the industry and demand that I grasp the kind of real estate knowledge that went well beyond convincing a young couple to rent an apartment.

Could I do it?

Expert Training

It's probably true of many professions. You get a taste of something that interests you, and initially, you achieve some success. Then you reach a point where an enormous leap of faith must be taken. After fretting about the CPM requirements, I made up my mind and told myself, "Glenn, it's time to be trained by the experts."

Earning my CPM was not strictly academic. Although I did coursework and then took exams to determine my level of knowledge, making the grade also included increasing the size of my portfolio—the properties I managed, having a certain number of years in the industry, learning to write management plans, and working under another CPM. But nothing was guaranteed. The student needed to be nominated to have the opportunity to assist an experienced property manager.

My instructors had decades of real estate experience and spoke the lingo. The terminology thrilled me—yield, cash flow analysis, return on investment, and on and on. I processed an avalanche of new insights and, at times, was not always sure I would survive. But I set my mind to studying it, learning it, practicing the principles, and lo and behold, I eventually got good at it.

It took me five years to earn my credentials, and that was fine with me because, in the meantime, I enjoyed incremental advancements.

When a third building was added to my responsibilities with the Shadow Mountain group, I finally achieved my goal of becoming a regional manager. Not bad for a guy who started by taking out the garbage. I stayed with that company for another couple of years before accepting a more challenging position and moving away from Utah.

It was wonderful to be gainfully employed while studying, learning, and meeting generous industry professionals. I lived and breathed property management and may have been happy to continue in that capacity if, as you now know, my wife hadn't challenged me to become an owner and reap the benefits (and a few headaches).

When it finally happened, when I took ownership of

a small apartment complex that would eventually yield a delicious profit, I turned a corner and never looked back.

Yet the circumstances that surrounded this shift in my life were somewhat unusual. An extremely wealthy and wise real estate investor provided an opportunity that I never could have predicted. The lessons, learned quickly and profoundly, expanded my understanding of the rewards and risks involved.

Through it all, I was reminded that success in the real estate industry is less about money than it is about people. By jumping in and getting involved, I developed relationships that would continue to guide me toward my ultimate goals.

GLENNISM #2:
SPEAK TO YOUR BOSS

If I had not spoken up and shared my aspirations with my boss, where would I be today? She gave me my first opportunities to sink or swim. She also provided excellent guidance at a key moment in my life. Holding it all in may be necessary now and then. But by talking out loud and seeking help, I learned the reality of what I must do to achieve my dreams.

NOTES AND THOUGHTS

_____

_____

_____

_____

_____

_____

_____

_____

_____

THREE

CHARACTER DEVELOPMENT

In Utah, I'd improved my resume by moving up the food chain with small companies. Once I'd earned my CPM designation, I was promoted from regional manager to director of operations. And yet, restless and hungry for even bigger challenges, I enlisted the help of a headhunter who began to look for opportunities nationwide.

I landed in Seattle, where I joined a group called Equity Residential. My new employer was a REIT—real estate investment trust—that owned 230,000 apartments. Moving from a small firm to one of the nation's largest was a big step that opened a fantastic chapter in my life.

Once again, I took on the role of regional manager in a territory with 10,000 units. The scope of the assignment was, of course, expansive. What made it formative and memorable was my boss, Kari. She was a great leader who loved to teach and train with a process called a 360-degree personal evaluation. It was one of the most enlightening experiences of my life.

The process was a deep dive into myself that revealed personality traits I didn't even know I had. It felt as though I was peeling back layers of an onion to discover my strengths and weaknesses and how I was perceived by my bosses, peers, and employees.

You might wonder why Kari and Equity Residential would take the time and spend the money to put us through all this. Finally, I realized the company knew we would become better people, better leaders. The evaluation was an investment in a guy named Glenn Gonzales and many others. It moved me.

At the same time, I realized it was a smart business move. The managers would benefit, but so would the company. That's another reason I teach my maintenance people and property managers as much as possible. All ships must rise in the harbor, not just the big ships.

Kari's impact on my life didn't end with the 360-degree evaluation. She told me point blank that if I was going to be a respected member of this profession, I must be all in, completely committed. In her opinion, that meant getting involved with the Washington Multi-Family Housing Association (WMFA) that she belonged to. There was an element of networking inherent in the gatherings, but it was also educational—experienced people sharing what they had learned through the years.

I must confess, my initial reaction was not positive, especially when she told me that everyone volunteered. Frankly, I didn't want to sit on committee and gab. It struck me as a waste of time. I needed those unpaid hours to meet my job and family responsibilities.

I was wrong.

As soon as I got involved, I understood why Kari had insisted I contribute. It was a tremendous opportunity to sit across the table from men and women with decades of experience who could mentor me—outside of my job environment. They weren't my boss, and they weren't my employee. They were my teachers, and soon, they became my peers. This is how I came to meet a man who was instrumental in helping me buy my first property.

John Gibson sat on the WMFA board of directors and was highly advanced in his career and extremely successful. Our paths intersected during board meetings and discussions, and I looked up to him.

I was highly impressed and motivated by John's success. I knew I wanted to buy property, but I didn't quite know how or where to start. I'd been looking for small properties and found a 60-unit deal in Tacoma. I put the numbers together as best I could from an operating budget perspective and then asked John if he would give me some feedback. He generously agreed. But his response to the property surprised me.

"Glenn, I'm going to be honest with you. It's an okay deal and would probably work out for you. But I've got a better deal for you," he said.

John went on to describe a 44-unit apartment building that he owned but described as "very dysfunctional." It was poorly managed.

At first, this didn't make sense to me. John was a seasoned veteran who understood the need for excellent oversight of his real estate portfolio. I had to ask, "Well, if you own it, why isn't it managed well?"

"Glenn, I have a brand-new 400-unit property that I'm building from the ground up. I've got to keep my eyes on that prize. The smaller building is just not worth my time."

Oh my, wouldn't I love to be in that position? I promised myself that someday I would be.

John invited me to look at the property after telling me that he would be willing to carry 100 percent of the note. That meant he would play the role of the bank so that I wouldn't have to go looking for a loan. Then he said, "All I'll need from you is a $150,000 down payment."

That's when reality smacked me in the face. I didn't have that kind of money. But was I willing to let a little problem like that break a great deal? No. I turned to colleagues in the WMFA.

Scott was a power washing contractor I'd contracted with to maintain some of the properties I managed. I pitched the project to him.

He asked, "How much are we talking?"

I explained that he would need to invest $75,000 to be part of a three-way cut that would include another investor and me.

"Glenn, how much money is the other investor putting in?"

"The other investor will put in $75,000, and you'll put in $75,000."

The numbers were not making sense to him.

"I don't get it. How much money are *you* putting in?"

"Zero."

"Glenn, how does that math work?"

That was a fair question. I reminded Scott that I had brought him a great opportunity that would require a financial investment but very little of his time. I would arrange the purchase and manage the renovation that we'd need to do. When I'd visited the building, I found a quirky place that functioned a bit like an old hotel. It was obvious to me what needed to be done. The rents were way too low for the neighborhood because the building couldn't compete with other properties nearby. By upgrading kitchens and baths and making magic with the curb appeal, we'd quickly improve cash flow.

Then I told him Kari was the second investor. She

didn't blink an eye when I asked if she would join me. It was gratifying and reassuring that a professional of her experience would commit. Again, her money was one thing. Her industry experience added even more value.

Done deal, right? No, there were more twists to this improbable tale.

When I went back to John and told him I had the $150,000, he said he did not want the money. Rather, he told me to use every dollar to renovate the building. At first, I was surprised. Then I realized how smart he was.

If John was going to carry the note—a large sum of money, even for an old property in need of repair—he wanted to make sure I had enough working capital to fix the problems so that the building could finally become profitable.

John's approach was common back in the day. It's called a wrap-around mortgage. He already had a bank loan, so once the building was renovated and collecting rent, I'd make a payment to John, who would then make his mortgage payment.

If, on the other hand, I had assumed his loan and then defaulted, that would have been a black mark on both our records. He avoided that by using the wrap-around concept.

His strategy included one more shrewd decision. Even if I'd defaulted on my monthly payments, and he had to resume control of the property, he would receive an improved, partially renovated apartment building that he had not paid one dollar for. Smart.

Thankfully, we fixed up the broken apartments, raised rents, quickly attracted tenants, and the investment began to make money.

The word millionaire has always resonated with Americans. Perhaps its luster has been dimmed a little with the emergence of the billionaire class. But for most citizens in this great nation, *millionaire* still shimmers and resonates. I know it does for me.

Imagine how moved I was when we sold our building for a million dollars more than we'd paid for it. Granted, not all the money came to me, a former maintenance man. Yet together, we had achieved a million-dollar victory.

Gratification was also found in the fact that my investors made well beyond their initial $75,000 contribution. It is one thing to fill your own pockets. But I've got to tell you, when you also make money for other people, the joy is huge.

Let's review. I profited from my first property even though I did not have the $150,000 needed for a down payment. Also, the deal didn't come to me by searching through listings in a newspaper or online. Good fortune came to me because I'd volunteered with the WMFA, an organization that was all about sharing and teaching.

I'd also chosen a mentor. I hadn't just asked John to look over a deal I was considering in Tacoma; I'd asked if he would guide me, and he agreed. Yet, his decision was also based on the time we spent on the WMFA board of directors. I'd been elected treasurer of the board, and he appreciated my contribution to the meetings. It was apparent to him that I was serious and would eventually succeed.

Does it feel like we're on the verge of another *Glennism*? I'll hold off for now, but what proverb comes to your mind? What lesson have you learned?

Sometimes I look back on that miracle and shake my head. My goodness. My first project was profitable, and yet I had no experience.

Then I stop and remind myself that's not true. I had no experience purchasing and owning a property, but I did bring a lot to the ballgame. My years in maintenance and management had given me an eye for what needed to be done to that old place. I was not a wealthy man then, but I had the know-how to manage that project, to steer the ship into port. Never undervalue your contribution. (Sorry. That sounds like a Glennism.)

Learning: The Flip Side

I've always wondered why wise men and women rarely say, "We learn from our successes." Instead, they focus on mistakes as teachable moments. I learned why when it came time to sell our property.

When a buyer for our small apartment building

stepped forward, we were able to settle with John so that he was "made whole," which is a real term meaning he got all his money back. That left the three of us, Kari, Scott, and I, with a decision to make. Our buyer had a loan for about two-thirds of our asking price but also needed us to do as John had done—carry the remaining portion of the debt as a loan.

We agreed to do so because it meant we could move forward with the sale. It was pragmatic and maybe a little bit altruistic. And it was a big mistake.

The buyer made several payments to us, and then he stopped. Shortly thereafter, he also stopped making payments on his banknote. If he defaulted on the bank loan, it would create a loss on the profit the three of us had made on the sale.

Are we having fun yet?

Those were unhappy days. Victory had been snatched from our grasp due to a foolish decision. When you go to college, you expect to pay tuition, right? Well, it looked like I was going to pay a lot of tuition to learn these real estate lessons.

But I refused to give up. I returned to my WMFA colleagues and explained my predicament. Eventually, someone knew someone who bought notes that were about to default. I dialed the phone number and fell into conversation with a man named Ed. Little did I know then how important this relationship would become in later years.

Why would Ed agree to buy a loan that was about to go bust? His offer was 60 cents on the dollar. If, for example, the loan was a million dollars, Ed would acquire it for only $600,000. That's a bargain. Is there still risk involved? Absolutely. But in real estate, I was learning that one man's ceiling is another man's floor. Ed acquired the banknote and saved the day. My partners and I would not lose our entire profit. All we had to do was make up the 40 cents per dollar discount that allowed Ed to take custody of the loan.

In the end, we lost about half our profit. Even then, we were feeling good. Scott and Kari had done well on their investments, and Mr. Maintenance Man, who had not spent a penny of his own money, was also sitting pretty.

And I still had my day job to count on.

Until I didn't.

After several years with Equity Residential, I left for a job that paid me a lot more money. I was pleased with my salary for several months until I realized the company that provided property management services was making promises to real estate owners that they couldn't keep. This was a cardinal sin, in my opinion. Excellent management was necessary to keep commercial real estate profitable. We were failing our clients if we could not deliver the kinds of services that protected investors. I couldn't live with that.

I contacted the headhunter who'd helped me find

my previous job, and within a few months, he found me another position. Although the company was located in Palo Alto, California, they had a Seattle office, so I did not have to relocate. But I did have to change hats and see things from the flip side of the owner/manager relationship.

The California company bought distressed properties, fixed them up, and added them to their portfolio. They were owners, not property managers. My new job demanded that I adopt the mindset of an asset manager. It was a whole new perspective that taught me how to view property through the lens of ownership. I learned about risk, appreciation, finance, value, cost control—all the things an owner must master. Ironically, my responsibilities also included hiring property management companies for each complex.

I loved the job because my knowledge was growing so much. By then, I'd been in the industry for about 15 years, and I can honestly say I never became complacent. I learned everything I could in whatever position I held. I wanted to be good—really good. I wanted to be the best.

The impulse to learn through experience was challenged about three years later when a dark cloud began to cast its shadow over the global economy. I received a call from my boss in Palo Alto and didn't like what I heard. The crash of 2008 was upon us. Nothing lasts forever, apparently. All things must pass.

GLENNISM #3:
NO MONEY, NO PROBLEM

Money is both a motivator and a brick wall. Too often, we limit ourselves because we look at our bank accounts and determine, "I can't afford it." Change that thought. Refuse to let money shape your aspirations. Find ways to move forward in whatever you are doing by offering the Value of You. Yes, you are an asset to whatever future you can imagine. Begin to explore ways that everything you have now is enough—enough to allow you to move forward, from maintenance man/woman to millionaire.

NOTES AND THOUGHTS

_____

_____

_____

_____

_____

_____

_____

_____

FOUR

BOOM TO BARGAIN HUNTERS

Progress is sweet when you look around your modest kingdom and see that your kids are doing well in school, your spouse is happy, and together you are expanding your material wealth. Working for the Palo Alto company paid well, so we could buy a boat and enjoy time on the Puget Sound. Other toys like mountain bikes and a fancier car fit well into the spacious garage of our new home. The wind was in our sails. I felt as though I was at the top of my career.

Yet beneath the shimmering veneer of professional success was the hard truth of capitalism. To buy the car, a bigger home, and a boat, I needed bank loans. My wife Heidi and I certainly qualified because we had a solid credit rating.

And at work, we were steaming ahead full throttle by renovating large apartment complexes and raising rents

MAINTENANCE MAN TO MILLIONAIRE

to improve our cash flow. There did not seem to be any reason why we could not keep growing and prospering. Then, in 2008, I watched the stock market crisis unfold on television. Every day, CNBC and other financial channels had terrible news to report. It was alarming and felt as if somebody was throwing rocks at our glass house. At first, I did not think it could affect large companies like my employer. I was wrong.

In the years before the mortgage market crashed, the price of real estate, in some regions, was soaring. For buyers of single-family homes, rising prices and the ecstasy of a "boom town" economy caused them to bid out of fear: If they didn't get into the market then, when would they have a shot at owning a home? And banks were making it easy to get a loan or several loans with variable rates to accommodate the hunger to grab hold of the American Dream at nearly any cost.

I already had a nice home. But in those "hot" market years, my goal was to expand my own real estate portfolio with rental homes. The idea had become common in those days: Let somebody else pay the mortgage. Sounds good, unless, of course, the occupant can no longer afford to pay the rent.

The initial wake-up call came when one of our three rental homes became vacant. We couldn't quickly find another tenant, and we didn't have ample ancillary cash to cover the shortfall because we were stretched with our own mortgage and loans for cars and toys. So, I used a credit card to cover the rent.

Then, a second home went vacant. This time, we lowered the rent and found an occupant, but the money was not enough to cover our mortgage payment. I began to panic.

Each of our rentals had required a down payment of about $50,000 each. With that much money at risk, we decided to reduce our burden by selling the properties. We quickly got offers, but they were too low, much lower than our bank loans. This was truly frightening. Our financial stability was taking a serious hit.

But let's pause here to gain some perspective.

As terrifying as our situation was, our pain was someone else's gain. One person's ceiling is another person's floor, right? Guess who was bidding on our properties?

Bargain hunters. Maybe they were couples who had not been able to afford a home a few years earlier or had wisely stayed on the sidelines as home prices inflated. Or maybe they were members of a consortium that had ample cash to take advantage of falling real estate values. Whatever. A lot of people got hurt in the market crash, including veterans who had millions of dollars tied up in leveraged properties. Yet, the downturn also began a new cycle of bargain buying.

When the offers for our three properties were far too low to pay our mortgages, I called our loan officer to discuss the dilemma. Heidi and I were not the only investors seeking solutions. In the end, our banker agreed to a short sale on three of our four properties.

Short sale is a real estate term that describes liquidating a distressed property below the amount of the mortgage. The laws surrounding these transactions differ in various states. In some cases, banks may forgive the gap, and while that may sound lucky, it comes with a price. We lost all of our down payment money, and our credit rating was ruined. We got nothing out of the rental portfolio that was supposed to grow through the coming years. The turn of events was a painful setback.

But the sale of those properties did not end our worries.

My boss in Palo Alto called one day to tell me that the company was also struggling. The big ten brands in the Seattle area, including Boeing and Microsoft, had laid off thousands of employees as the mortgage crisis spread. The ripple effect meant jobless occupants were forced to seek low-cost housing. The ability to raise rents was gone, and so my employer was losing equity and forced to cut back expenses. I was an expense they could no longer afford.

Negotiating Survival

At first, I was rattled by the words, "We have to lay you off." Oh my goodness, after all that had happened to my investments, did I also have to suffer the indignity of unemployment?

Once the shock wore off, I asked my boss for a meeting and made her an offer.

"I understand why you laid me off, but you still need somebody to do all my work, right?"

"Yes."

I offered to stay on temporarily but with a 50 percent salary cut.

"Why would you do that?" she asked.

First, I did not intend to go back full-time. Half pay translated into a workweek of about 20 to 25 hours. The remaining time would be used to search for a new job. I knew that it was better to be employed while interviewing for another position.

My boss accepted the offer, and I'd negotiated myself from zero cash flow to a 50 percent paycheck. It was better than nothing, even though reducing my pay was not a sustainable strategy. To salvage what we could from the wreckage caused by our spending habits and a historic market event, Heidi and I began to sell everything we owned. The boat and other toys had to go, but, once again, we were at the mercy of bargain hunters.

Selling our primary home became our next goal, even though we knew what kind of real estate environment we were trapped in. Our recent history also limited our options. Since the bank had already agreed to a short sale on three of our rentals, they would not approve that course for our dwelling. We had to accept a foreclosure, and that put an even larger black mark on our credit rating.

Heidi and I were in shock. We sat together and pondered how we could have let all this happen. Our good fortune had collapsed and put us in a predicament President Abe Lincoln had faced and eloquently described:

> *"I have been driven many times upon my knees by*
> *the overwhelming conviction that*
> *I had nowhere else to go."*
> **— Abraham Lincoln**

Yes, we got on our knees and prayed. That process led us to review our beliefs and habits. Our church leaders had always advised us to save for a rainy day and avoid living beyond our means. We had failed to follow their counsel. So, when the rain came, we were not prepared.

Daily Standards

After mourning our losses, we had the good sense to ask ourselves, what are we going to do differently? First, we would simplify our lives. This was not a hard decision to come by. After all, we had lost or sold most of our possessions. More to the point, we were determined to keep things simple even when our financial picture began to improve. We would take the advice of the many wise money advisors we'd read who encouraged us to live well below our means.

Aside from those personal decisions, through the years, I'd also developed what I called *Glenn Standards*. The first standard, "Show that you care," came to me in Seattle when Equity Residential provided excellent training and personal growth opportunities. The other standards also grew out of my experiences with John Gibson and other veteran real estate investors. I believed that if I abided by these guidelines, they would keep me on course throughout the next stages of my career. I still glance at them often:

Glenn's Standards

Show that you care

Team empowerment

Attention to detail

Never give up

Do it now

Accountability

Raise the bar

Don't be good; be great

Stick to the plan

About three months after agreeing to a cut in my salary, I found another opportunity. An acquaintance I'd met some years before had moved to Austin, Texas and founded an acquisitions firm. He had fired a couple of property management companies that he said were not doing a "good job." His plan was to let go of his current management firm if I would agree to join him to create and implement a solid management plan for his properties. The offer also included a 35 percent share of ownership.

All of the above sounded like a great next step. Heidi and I loaded all our remaining belongings into one U-Haul trailer and began our journey south. In Austin, we found a small, single-family home we could afford to rent and began to settle in.

It did not take long for me to realize I had been misled. The Austin company did not have a management company in place, there was no operating manual, and the employees had no meaningful leadership and were, therefore, doing everything backward.

The man who had offered me the partnership had also filed lawsuits against a couple of management companies, and there were liens filed against a few of his properties. He was in trouble, and I did not want to be partner to the troubles he had created.

"Look," I told him, "I'll stay on for a year to clean up the management mess, but I'm not going to become a partner unless we can put these problems behind us."

Once again, I combined all my experiences, worked my magic, and turned the whole portfolio around. My success allowed me to assume 35 percent ownership, and I was president of the property management wing of the company.

Meanwhile, my financial status was on the rise again, and Heidi and I shared a sense of relief. We were free of debt, and our income had improved so that we could begin to save money for future ventures. The next twist in my path from maintenance man to millionaire came sooner than we had expected.

My partner had the opportunity to buy a 201-unit property in San Antonio that would soon foreclose. After he declined the opportunity, a banker called me to ask if I was interested in managing the apartment complex. I visited the site and then proposed that all would be well if the bank would invest $1 million into the multifamily property. I'd manage the renovation and bring operations back to normal, and they would eventually be able to sell the foreclosed real estate at a profit.

They didn't like that idea.

"No way. We're a bank. We don't invest; we lend."

This was true, of course. Investing was risky. They had just foreclosed on a property and did not want to suffer any more losses. Could I scoop up the deal and turn it around? At that point, I certainly didn't have that kind of money or equity to play with. But I did have lots of knowledge and past experiences that began whispering in my ear: "No money, no problem."

Remember how John Gibson in Seattle had agreed to carry the note for his dysfunctional property if I would spend the $150,000 down payment on repairs? Couldn't that same concept work in this situation, even though this was a much bigger deal?

I called the banker I'd spoken to and told him I had another idea. "If I put in a million bucks, would you carry the note on the property?"

His reply was enthusiastic. "That's a great idea!" Then he asked, "Do you have a million?"

"No." I could feel his spirit sink. That changed when I added, "But I know people who do."

Why did this proposal succeed, whereas the first one was rejected? Isn't the bank still risking a million dollars?

Yes, in a sense. But my second approach gave the bank an opportunity to do what they do best: loan, not invest.

My search for the million dollars began with a colleague I'd met through the years. He saw value in the San Antonio property, and together, we began to raise money from local investors.

This unexpected deal was doubly sweet for me. It would put me back on the map as a buyer and investor, and by adding it to the portfolio of properties I managed in Austin, that company would grow a little bigger. Or so I thought.

When I spoke to my co-owner and told him my plan, he said, "You're not allowed to do that."

I was surprised. "What do you mean?"

"Our agreement includes a no-compete clause."

"Compete? I'm not starting my own management company. I'm bringing the San Antonio complex into our management company. You'll benefit from it."

He repeated his objections and threatened to fire me. This made no sense to me.

"You can't fire me. I'm a part-owner, and I'm helping grow the company."

In the end, the man who had invited me to Austin kicked me out of the firm and filed a lawsuit against Heidi and me. This forced me to sink or swim. His decision to push me out was the best thing that ever happened to me.

Is the moral of the story to never invest in real estate? No. The moral is never to be surprised by other people's behavior and illogic. Protect yourself. Know your rights. Follow the standards I shared earlier.

Fortunately, the adversity that clouded my future in Austin arrived with a silver lining. The money I'd made on the San Antonio property provided a small nest egg. In the short time we'd been in Texas, Heidi and I had been able to save for a rainy day.

The steps we took next were discussed in detail and carefully mapped out. If we failed, we'd be right back where we started when we arrived in the Lone Star State.

But if we succeeded…

GLENNISM #4:
DON'T BE GOOD; BE GREAT

When you consider the lives of people you admire, what do you see in them? My heroes in business are the men and women who took a leap. They did something that many people may wish for but didn't have the guts to do. It's simple: Those people in the spotlight decided that being good at something was not good enough. Greatness can be defined in many ways. For me, it meant ownership, not just of property but my path in life, my manhood, my destiny.

NOTES AND THOUGHTS

_____

_____

_____

_____

_____

_____

FIVE

OVERCOMING OBSTACLES

Before arriving in Texas, Heidi and I had made the decision to live well below our means for the first time in our marriage. That step taught us the important distinction between a need and a want. I might want a new car, but do I need it? We may want a bigger house, but do we need it? This simple principle helped us define a unique way of life. We began to thrive.

Our discipline allowed us to save and create a modest nest egg. Then, the successful San Antonio deal expanded that fund. You already know that putting some money aside helps to endure rainy days. But it might also be used to brighten the future.

When I was booted from my partnership in Austin, I was out of a job, but had stumbled into a unique opportunity that gave me two clear choices.

One: I could search for another job. I'd done it before. Maybe calling my headhunter would be the best way to go.

But if I found a job, it would mean that I was once again "working for the *Man*." That wasn't entirely bad. Through the years, I'd been paid to learn about real estate. It was like a scholarship. I'd made a good living, and I'd developed skills and a reputation that had brought me a lot of respect from the community.

And yet, I'd also been laid off a couple of times due to circumstances and personalities that were beyond my control. The memory of those times motivated me to consider a different path.

Two: I could be my own boss. I had mastered my craft through hard work and passion for the industry. If I could take all that I had learned to finally build my own property management and ownership business, the *Man* I'd be working for would be me.

I was at a tremendous crossroads in my life. Adversity had put pressure on me to stay the course or make a big change.

After doing some calculations, we decided that the money we'd saved would buy me about one year to make my own luck. It was not an easy decision. But we'd arrived at a point in our lives where we had to wonder: If not now, when? It was the right time to be self-employed.

We knew I couldn't do it alone. For starters, I'd need to choose a trustworthy partner. My new status would also demand that I reach out to past relationships in search of deals and find investors who might help acquire new properties.

Considering all that had to be done just to begin, I was overwhelmed—even though it was thrilling to basically write myself a check so that I could rise every day to pursue my most passionate interests.

One of the early calls I made was to a man in California who once employed me to manage his property. After describing my new venture, he agreed to sell me his apartment complex.

Then, I got a call from a banker in Austin who had hired me to manage several foreclosures while I was still employed. He had an interesting tale to tell.

"Glenn, since you left your job, those properties you were managing for us aren't doing as well. Would you and your new company have any interest in acquiring those complexes?"

I jumped at the chance. "Yes. I'm very interested."

Don't think the phone was ringing off the hook. Every day, I had to do the real estate hustle, otherwise known as working the phones and shaking hands. Yet, the more I did seemed to bring me more opportunity because word spread that I had my own enterprise.

My next new property came after I called a man who'd sold me a lot of property insurance over the years. I simply asked if he was aware of anyone who was ready to sell their commercial real estate holdings. Again, fate was on my side.

"I know a guy in San Antonio who wants to sell a 300-unit apartment complex. Do you want me to set up a lunch meeting?"

Yes, please.

Our meeting went so well that we struck a deal while still at lunch. Now I had several properties under my wing, but there was one thing missing: investors.

Asking for money can be intimidating, depending on your mindset. When you are employed by an established, reputable company, you have some confidence because a little of the brand's prestige rubs off on you. When you are self-employed, you don't yet have a large banner to wave in the wind. You wonder if you'll be taken seriously.

I was pleasantly surprised to learn that my management successes over the years had earned me some respect. The people I called knew my background and saw me as a real estate *expert*. They didn't care that I was self-employed. It was my knowledge and track record that gave them confidence to do business with me.

As it turned out, this new phase of my career was rejuvenating. I learned that I had more than a resume. I was trusted by a circle of peers who knew that all my endeavors were guided by strong principles.

But throughout the first year of building my business, a lawsuit filed by my former partner lingered. In my worst moments, I feared that defending myself would rip a hole in my finances and reputation.

Then, more than a year after being fired, I received some encouraging news. Unfortunately, it arrived at about the same time Heidi and I were facing a life-and-death predicament.

Houston, We Have a Problem

A weight was lifted when I learned that the court had dismissed my partner's lawsuit. Although I'm not allowed to disclose the specifics, I was happy with the settlement, which was helpful to me. I was liberated from the dark legal cloud that had followed me into my new life.

Also, in this same period, I sold the 200-unit property that had started all the troubles with my partner. My return on that investment one year after making the purchase was four times the amount of my annual salary. The leap Heidi and I had made was working out. I was the captain of my own ship. Yet even as we received those blessings, I was forced to contend with a much more profound threat to my future: my wife was dying.

Heidi's health had declined to the point where she weighed 85 pounds, needed a wheelchair, and relied on oxygen tanks 24 hours a day. Both lungs were failing her, and without a double lung transplant, she was doomed.

In June of 2015, after consulting with pulmonary specialists, Heidi was put on a lung transplant list. We were told that it could take six months to a year before a match was available. The news shook us. We both knew she would be lucky to survive three months. We sought other opinions in Houston and flew to Denver to meet another specialist with the hope that we might find a faster medical solution. No go. Heidi's days were numbered.

I was angry and desperate and didn't want to let her go. God was the target of my fury—"You can't take my wife from me!"

But after seeking blessings from church friends and counsel from friends and family, the prognosis remained the same. I was at the lowest ebb of my emotional struggle. Heidi and I had begun to discuss funeral arrangements, a conversation that no one wants to have with their beloved spouse, who is far too young to die. I finally surrendered. The outcome would be His will, not mine.

On July 3rd, 2015, I stood before our church and publicly declared my change of heart and mind.

"If He wants to take her home, I'm telling you, that's hard for me. I've fought it, but if He has a plan for my wife in the hereafter, if that's what He wants, I have to trust Him."

The experience helped unburden me, even as I grieved for Heidi, her fate, and the loss we would suffer.

On July 7th, we got a call from the hospital. They'd found a double-lung match.

This miracle was humbling and immediately demanding. Since the transplant would happen at the Houston Medical Center, and we had no idea how long recovery would take, I had to find an apartment that would accommodate Heidi and me, as well as our parents—mine would fly in from California, Heidi's from Utah—and our children, all of whom would help with the 24-hour care that would be needed after surgery if everything went our way.

I leased an apartment near the hospital but felt the crush of too many responsibilities. With so little time, how could I possibly move furniture and our essential belongings while also supporting Heidi and running a business that was flourishing?

On the night when the complicated surgery began, I was in the waiting room all alone because everything had happened so fast. I didn't have time to call family and friends and ask if they could be with me. My heart was with Heidi, but my mind was racing with all the major business decisions that needed my attention if our business was to succeed. I felt overwhelmed and unprepared for the collision of my personal and professional responsibilities.

Then, as my internal battled intensified, two women approached me and asked why I was alone. After I'd explained my circumstances, they surprised me by saying, "Would you like us to pray for you?"

MAINTENANCE MAN TO MILLIONAIRE

"Yes. Please."

These two angels sat with me, and suddenly, I didn't feel alone anymore. Certainly, the warmth of these two compassionate strangers moved me. But in that moment, I also felt carried by the abundant love of our savior and was immediately comforted in my time of need.

By morning, the surgeons informed me that the transplant had gone well. So well, in fact, that Heidi would spend only a week in the intensive care unit, then another week in recovery before moving to our Houston apartment. Hallelujah.

Fabulous news, of course. But I was exhausted. I drove to the apartment, ready and willing to sleep on the floor. When I opened the door, I was stunned to find a completely furnished, functional living space.

Before the surgery, I'd expressed my concerns to friends at church. They said, "Don't give it another thought. We'll take care of everything."

They'd gone to my landlord to get a set of keys and then began setting things up. They moved in furniture—all the beds were made with linens and bedspreads—appliances and all the usual household goods, tissue, laundry detergent, and food. After expressing my predicament, donations of all kinds poured in, and the blessings of the congregation were apparent, not just in Houston, but in Austin as well. Friends mowed our lawn and collected the mail that was piling up at the house we'd abandoned when the lung match was found.

Two weeks later, Heidi was moved to the apartment. Her medication schedule was constant and complicated. Everything, food and medicine, had to be crushed or pureed, then poured through a feeding tube. My mother was a retired nurse, so she took command of those procedures and taught each of us what to do when it was our turn to watch over our beloved Heidi.

There was another complication. Business was booming. It sounds crazy to complain. I was living my dream, right? Yes, that was true. But as I walked a tightrope between entrepreneurial goals and domestic life, I had to accept—again—that catastrophe and success don't necessarily arrive when it is convenient.

A week after my wife's surgery, I submitted an offer on a 650-unit complex called Montecito Creek in Dallas that was the largest deal of my career. When Heidi was unconscious, I was working and making deals. When she was conscious, I was bedside holding her hand. I didn't talk about business or tell her how hard it had all been because she didn't need any more stress in her life. The only thing that caused her alarm was that I had my hands on our checkbook and was paying our bills.

"That's my job."

"I know, but—"

"Don't mess it up, fellah."

Even when severely weakened, she had a sense of humor.

The deal closed September 29ᵗʰ for $35 million. A couple of weeks later, we returned to Austin, though Heidi was still on a feeding tube and struggled to walk more than 200 yards per day—doctor's orders. With so many blessings, there was nothing to do but fall to my knees in humble gratitude. God was looking down on me.

Our company quickly grew to 4,000 apartment units under ownership. The management company that had let me go only had 4,200 units. Here I was nearly as large as and more profitable than my previous job.

Water Bottle Lesson

Once Heidi's crisis had passed, I could look back and ask, what kept me going? At another time, I might have dropped my goal of being an entrepreneur and grabbed a normal job. It would have seemed more stable. And we needed stability. The money from the real estate deals may sound grand, but the stress created from the many details involved could rattle a guy. And then, after taking possession of a property, you must manage it well.

My answer to my own question was "inspiration." I was inspired by the way the lung match and surgery happened. The support we received from friends, family, and our church was also inspirational; there was no way I could have carried all that stress alone. The business side of things was also an inspiration. The fulfillment of deals coming to me, despite the circumstances, provided a reason to believe in our new way of life.

As a result, I had a tremendous desire to pay it forward and help others. More than any other time in my life, I took notice of other people's needs and did what I could to help. Sometimes that meant helping the employees I would eventually bring into my business. Or maybe it meant reaching out to someone in church or in banking, and so on. Our blessings accumulate by the simple act of giving. Sometimes the giving is merely a change in attitude.

As Heidi's health improved, I noticed that she still had the habit of opening a small bottle of water, drinking about half, leaving the bottle somewhere in the house, and then later, opening another bottle. Before the surgery, it would annoy me that I'd find these bottles all over the place.

"Honey, why can't you just finish one bottle before you open another?" I'd ask. This usually ignited an argument. Pet peeves accumulate in every marriage, I suppose.

That's why I smiled the day I realized that the plastic bottles didn't bother me anymore. They provided a moment of comfort and joy. They made me grateful that

Heidi was still around. The things we all argue about are so insignificant when compared to the big picture.

Heidi is now physically healthier than ever because she was diligent about following her post-operation recovery plan. And I'm healthier, emotionally and spiritually. The stress and drama didn't ruin me but made me a better husband. I hold my wife's hand more often and daily remind her how happy I am that she survived the ordeal.

"I'm really grateful you're here–even when you open too many water bottles."

"Thanks, hon. Now take out the garbage."

GLENNISM #5:
EVERY DISASTER IS AN OPPORTUNITY

When times are tough, it is difficult to count our blessings. Fear takes over, and the road to recovery seems impossible. Yet, in my case, a sudden job loss also opened a door to new possibilities. I didn't run right through and begin a new venture. It took time and lots of talks with Heidi to find my way. Consider the main challenges in your life. On the one hand, troubles can feel terribly limiting. On the other, they may also be a clue to your real feelings or yearnings for change. Stand back from worry and get some objectivity. Search for at least one benefit that might come out of your adversity and make this process a habit whenever cloudy skies dim your view of life.

NOTES AND THOUGHTS

The adversity I faced in Stockton led me to all the knowledge I learned. Life is long and I have many years to put it to use. It led me to Kevin. It helped me find my true passion. The last buyer backed out but I know I will find a new buyer.

SIX

ASSEMBLING TRUST

Some people measure success by monetary things, and that's not necessarily success. Make a gain and enjoy a luxurious life, if that's what you want. At the same time, stay alert to problems that might be the result of your ambition. Do have you more headaches than ever before? Is your health declining? Do you have less time to unwind and enjoy time with your spouse and kids?

The constant need to grow and expand your finances does not always lead to a victory. In my experience, it can cause failure. There must be a balance in life and in business.

Years after Heidi survived her surgery, our business was growing in leaps and bounds. I no longer had one enterprise; I had several. There came a time when I needed to reset my priorities. I achieved this with the help of friends and colleagues at a church conference.

I also needed to visit my doctor because the rhythm

of my heart was erratic. Thankfully, a change in diet and adjusting the tempo of my life would resolve the problem. Later that day, I watched out my window as a massive storm moved into Austin. The sky broke open and unleashed a relentless downpour. But the wind was so fierce, the rain didn't just fall and flood the streets. It rushed horizontally as the lights in my house began to flicker. In my opinion, that's what happens when we lose objectivity and balance in business—things go sideways.

Fortunately, there are ways to keep things steady by broadening your view of life. It involves other people and fresh perspectives. I'll admit nothing in this world is perfect. Even this business method can go haywire. And yet, without it, most men and women will never achieve their biggest dreams.

External and Inner Circles

As you grow, you will need and want to grow a team. That may seem overwhelming at first. So, start simply by imagining the people you'd like to have around you to complete a single real estate transaction. You'll realize you already know men and women who have skills you can call on. You will also recognize gaps you need to fill.

Nothing happens all at once. Things evolve. Through the years, I've assembled a group of attorneys that have represented me on my loan documents, my purchase-sell agreements, title commitment reviews, and opinion letters. They've done at least 25 transactions for me. And since they now know me and the business so well, the process that was daunting in the beginning is now seamless. I'm grateful.

For example, the title company I mentioned has done at least 30 transactions for me. They've helped me when I was buying and selling. These experts know my schedule and how to contact me when documents must be signed.

Meanwhile, when I buy an apartment complex, I've got to renovate it. This means I must hire a general contractor to get in there and improve the property at a reasonable price. Fortunately, I've worked with the same general contractor for ten years, and he knows the color of paint we like to use, the carpet thread specifications, cabinet front, and countertops. He knows all of this because he's done thousands of them for me. And I keep him busy because I know he does quality work. This also means he gives me a break on total cost. It's a win-win. We both benefit.

I also have a bunch of brokers that I work with, as needed, to sell some of my deals or help me buy new deals. The loan brokers have been generous with their compliments. They have said, "Glenn, we like the professional, friendly way you conduct your business." So, you see, I'm not the only one choosing favorites. How we behave in the industry is noticed by others and respected if we give respect. They don't go out of their way to assist people who are difficult. Would you?

Your team might grow naturally simply by developing strong and loyal relationships at all levels. But are these people my employees? No. They are what I call my external team or circle, which consists of vendors, contractors, attorneys, and more.

My inner circle contains my employees and partners. This circle includes asset managers who I have hand-picked and people who have moved up through the ranks as our company grew, such as a transaction manager who initially joined us as an intern. Her story is among my favorite ways of doing business. She has evolved with the company because her understanding of our business and methods and culture runs deep.

Merely hiring talented people to join my inner circle is not enough. I must treat them right and reward them with bonuses and special events. Visits to excellent golf courses and all-expenses-paid cruises with their spouses were not something I could afford in the beginning. I'm overjoyed that we can share these experiences now because they help build trust and loyalty. A lot has been said about coaches and managers who have a knack for building positive cultures on athletic teams. The same is true of your business environment. Creating a portfolio of properties that enriches the company is a primary goal, but it is not the only purpose in life. Gifted people will stay and make important contributions if the atmosphere you create is supportive, fun, and respectful. I divide the workforce into two basic categories: people who get up and go to work because they must, and people who do great work because they want to.

Occasionally, I show my gratitude to an individual, not the entire team.

One morning an employee named Leslie called in to say that she would not be able to make it into the office. Instead, she would work at home.

I sensed some anxiety, so I asked, "You're home right now?" She was and assured me that she would be there all day. "Glenn, my car battery is dead, and I can't deal with it until later."

My gut response was to hop in my truck and drive to her home. When I got there, I pulled out my jumper cables and recharged her car battery by hooking it to my vehicle. Then, I took the keys to her car and told her I'd be back in a little while.

"Where are you going?"

"Do I look like the kind of guy who steals cars?"

I found a garage and had them install a new battery and change the oil. I also had them replace the wiper blades. Next, I drove to a car wash and had the car detailed.

A couple of hours later, I returned and tossed her the keys. "You won't have any more issues with your battery. You're fine."

She looked at her car and was quite aware that it had been shown some tender loving care. Speechless, her eyes filled with tears.

"Leslie, why are you crying?"

"Nobody does things like that. Why did you do that? You didn't have to do that."

She was right, in a way. But what she may not have realized is that I'd noticed that she always went the extra mile for me, working weekends and nights to fulfill bookkeeping chores that benefit my company. She was having one of those days, and I hoped a small gesture would lift her spirits.

"You have always worked so hard to produce good-quality work, Leslie. And I just wanted you to know how much I appreciate you."

I'm not congratulating myself. Sure, I genuinely wanted to help, but this kind of behavior is a smart way to build culture. It was unexpected, to be sure, and yet, in my opinion, it was also well-deserved. Did she owe me anything for my modest gift? No. She'd already paid me a thousand times by helping run my business smoothly. The Glennism here is obvious: building a culture and a productive work environment includes group activities and occasionally encouraging a valued individual who may be going through a tough patch.

Creating an attractive, productive culture is not only about special outings and financial bonuses. Your inner circle must always be challenged. Otherwise, the work might become mundane, and the team member becomes complacent. In that situation, an employee might show up for work only because he or she must feed their family. There's nothing wrong with being able to provide, but real estate is an excellent enterprise for growth. There is always more to learn, which can lead to promotions and expanding recognition of expertise. I believe it is fair to say that if you're working in this field and you're bored, there are a couple of explanations: This industry is not for you. Or you are not applying yourself and setting new goals each year. I may be the boss, but I love surrounding myself with ambitious, fair-minded people who are also guided by their own inner boss. These are the types of people who belong in my inner circle.

Finding Your Team

Start your team by making a list of your assets—friends, colleagues, service providers, your favorite waitress, or cashier at a store you frequent. We're attracted to people who engage and help us, so in a sense, I'm asking you to write down the names of people who make your life better and brighter. You can't necessarily offer them a job right now, and yet, you never know when you might need some input, advice, or a few minutes of brainstorming.

I often meet people I like and respect. Sometimes I wish I had a position to offer them, and, at other times, I make them an offer right on the spot.

When I met Mark, he was a banker who wanted to get involved in multifamily commercial real estate. Although he had dabbled in some small acquisitions, Mark knew he would benefit from having a mentor, which led to a mutual friend suggesting that he talk with me.

Lunch is almost never just lunch. Even the most casual meetings provide a window into someone else's life and soul. You may like what you see and sense that you could work together.

Mark had a full-time job with a bank and was in the Army Reserves. He was smart, personable, and receptive. At the time, NAPA was still a startup. We had survived our initial launch and then had a growth spurt. I had not expected to hire a new employee, but before lunch was over, I heard myself say, "Why don't you join us as an asset manager?"

His surprise was obvious. "But I don't know anything about that kind of work."

I appreciated his honesty. It was not his resume that had impressed me. I could tell we were both comfortable with each other, and I saw greatness in him. I believed he would learn fast if he had a mentor—namely, me.

Before he could join us, Mark owed the Army Reserve a month of service. I was willing to wait. When he finally walked through our doors, we rewarded him with his own desk—a black fold-up card table and an inexpensive phone we'd bought on sale at a big box office supply store. That was his first workstation. We couldn't afford anything fancier, and he didn't need it. He was in training. And we were a startup.

Mark began as an asset manager but grew into the role of director of operations. Over time, we found a way to use his strengths—his understanding of banking procedures and his gift for working with people to solve problems—to our advantage.

So, what was it that caused me to offer a job to Mark? It's a mix of intuition and fulfilling the practical needs of my enterprise.

For example, large companies that need employees may post an advertisement online and wait for resumes to arrive. That method probably works for many industries. It's straightforward, and every resume tells a story that can be developed further through the interview process. There are times when I may let colleagues know that I'm in need of a certain kind of person. And that message travels through a network of tight and loose connections.

More often, as you've probably noticed, good people seem to arrive as a natural consequence of me staying active and curious in my field of dreams and demonstrating a willingness to share. I welcome multiple points of view. I'm not seeking followers. Collaborators bring much more to the ballgame. Some may join my inner circle, while others are ideal external team members.

My contractor of choice is Danny, who was referred to me years ago. When we met, I was moved by the way he talked about his father, who had founded his company, and described how he and his brothers were determined to keep the family business afloat. He also told me about his wife and children. I was impressed with this man's work ethic and loyalty to family. I said to myself, "This is a guy I would like to do business with." Did I have to think about it for hours? No. Gut instinct.

Yet, there are common denominators when I reflect on meeting Mark, Danny, and others, including Leslie. I was and am attracted to their philosophy of life and their integrity. Loyalty and honesty are also part of the portrait. When these elements are combined, I'm inspired to say, yes, I want this person in my inner circle or included in my exterior team.

Can things go wrong? Yes.

Mark was, and is, a gifted person. I took him under my wing and worked with him side by side on everything I was doing. He was observing firsthand what I had learned after years of being in the industry. As we went forward, I showed him what I wanted him to do, how to do what I wanted him to do, and then I let him do it.

Like all human beings, Mark had his strengths and weaknesses. An asset manager must oversee the property management company we've hired to be sure they implement our asset management plan. The relationship can

become tense if the management company is not comply-
ing with our plan. Do you remember Glenn's Standards?
One of my main points is to *stick to the plan*. That's when
a hard conversation must happen and may lead to firing
one company and hiring another. Mark didn't like that
part of the job. He wanted to be everybody's friend.

Also, at one point, he fell behind in his work because
he was understandably overwhelmed by our fast expansion and acquisition of new properties. Rather than come
to me and ask for help or say, "Hey, I'm swamped here!"
he kept it under wraps until I became aware of the bot-
tleneck that was hindering our operation. Eventually, I
understood what had happened: Mark couldn't admit his
failure because he didn't want to disappoint me.

In a private conversation, I said, "Mark, it's okay to
raise your hand and ask for help."

"But that's an admission that, you know, I messed
up, or I'm underqualified."

"Not coming to me only creates a bigger problem.
Trust me, and I'll trust you to work it through if we're on
the same page."

Life is full of paradoxes. You're afraid to tell the boss
that something has gone wrong for fear that you'll be
criticized and demoted. Yet the boss loses confidence in
your ability if you're afraid to ask for help. Crazy, right?
When an employee or partner keeps a problem secret,
there is no way it can be resolved.

But even this difficult passage was a blessing in disguise. Mark was better suited to an operational role that demanded that he remain at his desk and not visit properties. In time, he helped improve our processes for engaging with banks, brokers, and management companies. He was excellent when working with spreadsheets and communicating with lenders. His effort created efficiencies that saved us time. And when we were presented with a new challenge, he was effective in finding a solution. I would throw tasks at him with no supervision or guidance, and he would develop a new system that was highly beneficial to our company. My confidence in him expanded.

When we first met, I saw greatness in Mark. Although he stumbled in one role, he has since proven his worth in a position that is better suited to his skill set and temperament. Do you sense a Glennism about to happen?

After bringing people together and doing everything possible to reward and encourage your inner circle and exterior team, how do you know you are succeeding?

Not long ago, I got a call from a man who'd worked for me in Austin before that partnership deteriorated, and I was forced out. This employee had become a friend, and now was seeking a new job because he'd been laid off. We chatted a bit before he told me his real reason for calling.

"While I was sorting out what I want to do next, making lists of pros and cons, remembering all the stress,

I kept coming back to our time working together. They were some of my best moments in the industry."

"Thank you. Do you know why you liked it so much?"

"Yeah. The environment."

"You mean the culture?"

He chuckled.

"Your favorite word. Yes, Glenn. It was the culture."

GLENNISM #6:

EXPAND YOUR PERSONAL LANDSCAPE

Self-reliance is important. But it only gets you so far and may lead to burnout. Building a team means you're not forcing yourself to shoulder the entire burden of success, which is impossible to do if you intend to grow. As you go about your day, keep track of the people you respond to, and jot down the qualities that impress you. Gut response, would you hire them if you had a job to offer? Even if you don't have a company yet, talk to these people. Get to know what they're all about. In that way, you're expanding your landscape and, who knows, maybe someday they'll offer the solution you've been looking for.

NOTES AND THOUGHTS

How do we balance trusting in partners if humans are un predictable? Letting partners in to our deal could jeopardize this deal if they fail to keep up their end of the deal, but are also ideal to grow.

SEVEN

OUT OF LOVE, IN THE KNOW

Don't fall in love; at least, not with a property. As the saying goes, love is blind. And when purchasing commercial real estate, you cannot afford to swoon or be wooed by a building that looks good but may not provide a nice return on the investment. You must do your homework and unearth every bit of useful data available so that you can make a well-informed, objective decision.

Another way of saying this is don't drink the Kool-Aid™.

We live in an age when there is an app for analyzing everything under the sun. And some experts claim their digital spreadsheets provide superior analysis. All I can say is, the numbers don't lie. Do some basic math, and if the numbers indicate a low return on a property you're considering, chances are you're going to get a low return.

There are exceptions, of course. When you've had 20 years of experience, you may buck the consensus and go with your gut.

MAINTENANCE MAN TO MILLIONAIRE

I'll give you an example. My company bought a deal in Lancaster, Texas, even though there were no data points. There was no reliable information because no one had renovated in the apartments in the surrounding area, so we could not make comparisons between one property and another. Regardless, my intuition told me that we had a unique opportunity, and we could afford to take on the risk. We eventually sold that deal for a fantastically high profit thanks to my informed gut response.

Until you have the experience, trust the data because, as soon as you say, "I love this deal and know it will work," you've become emotionally attached, and that can spell ruin. Love is blind.

I once worked with a man who insisted we buy a deal in Oklahoma. But after looking at the numbers, I said, "My friend, this is not a good deal."

He argued, "Yes, it is a good deal."

When I asked why, he replied, "Because I already have the debt and the equity lined up."

I told him, "Just because you found a lender and investors, it doesn't make it a good deal."

There were two other issues that I brought to his attention. We had no exit strategy, and he was comparing rents from the wrong neighborhood. I've told you before that the numbers don't lie. That is true unless you use the wrong numbers to justify your desires and intentions. Never ever become so emotionally attached to a deal that you begin to believe your own lies.

I persisted. "Look, you're not going to be able to raise the rents on these units."

"It's still a good deal," he insisted.

At the time, we were in acquisition mode. We needed to bring some new properties into our portfolio. After a long argument, I went against my better judgment and agreed to let him make an offer on the complex. My reward a year and a half later was bitter: we lost about $600,000 on that deal.

I'm not saying I'm always right. Things can go wrong, or inexperience can take you down a bumpy path. Remember, at the beginning of my career when I was prepared to buy a property in the Seattle area? Thank goodness, I asked for an opinion. My mentor, John Gibson, described the properties as merely "okay." Then he made me a better offer. I've never forgotten that lesson.

So, then why did I allow myself to buy the Oklahoma property? The answer to that question is better explored in a later chapter about partnerships. Sometimes, to get along in business, you must remain flexible—even at your own expense.

Over-the-Shoulder Mentoring

Everybody needs a coach, a mentor. I often speak with people who have questions about getting involved in real estate or a deal they have an eye on. Sharing information or teaching is a proud tradition in real estate and has been part of every job I've ever held. Show someone how you do what you do, and the world is a better, more prosperous place.

But if we had 90 days to work together, how would I coach you? That's the question a colleague asked during a conversation about real estate newbies. I knew I would not start with a bunch of lectures, despite my habit of offering Glennisms. Instead, I'd want to look over the shoulders of beginners and review the commercial property deals they were considering. In that way, I could ask some basic questions:

- How much is it going to cost?

- Are you going to raise your rents?

- Who's going to manage it? What's their reputation?

- Who is going to invest?

- What are your debt terms?

- Which lender are you going to for a loan?

- Who will do the renovation work, and how much will it cost?

This is only the beginning. There are a lot more questions I might ask, of course. But teaching is a lot more effective when a real situation is in the works. Theory is fine and is used in classrooms across the nation.

Hands-on or over-the-shoulder guidance is far superior.

So rather than ask all those questions of a student, I would suggest that he or she shadow me and follow me on every site visit, be part of every telephone conversation, and network with me at every professional event I attend.

This is why finding a mentor is important. And don't be afraid to ask for help. The real estate community is one of the most generous you could ever hope to join. My first important deal came after I asked an exceedingly experienced man who sat across from me at apartment association board meetings to look at the research I'd done. By doing so, I was asking for over-the-shoulder advice, and he delivered.

One important rule to remember when you finally request assistance: be respectful, listen and be grateful.

When reaching out, it is essential that you understand some commercial real estate lingo. There are many terms to absorb, so let's start with some of the most basic.

Letter of Intent (LOI)

Let's face it, commercial real estate documents can be complicated. To simplify, some buyers begin a deal with an LOI, which is a short document that explains the terms of the transaction.

Building Classifications

You'll think of the alphabet the first time you see

a reference to Class A, B, and C properties. There is also a Class D, but let's not go there. You may think you only want to work in Class A neighborhoods, but there are a lot of deals elsewhere. In short, the classifications are based on the age of buildings, locations, and types of amenities, such as on-site laundry, parking, pool, clubhouse, dog park, tennis courts, and workout facilities.

Common Area Maintenance (CAM)

I mentioned raising rents to create more profit. But how is the rent determined? It must include a base rent and an additional amount that is used to maintain a complex's common areas. All tenants use the sidewalks and parking areas, so rent might help pay for snow removal, outdoor lighting, insurance, and property taxes, etc.

Return on Investment

Who doesn't love ROI? It's what we're all looking for. The ROI measures the financial performance of a property. Is the return positive or negative? You calculate it this way: the return of an investment is divided by the cost of the investment. Your answer to that equation is a percentage or a ratio.

Cash flow divided by initial investment = ROI

Net Operating Income

This is all the revenue you receive from your property after subtracting operating expenses, the money needed to maintain the building. Your income will include rent, but don't forget CAMs, such as revenue from parking fees, laundry machines, etc. NOI is a before-tax sum, but it is also before debt service and capital expenses. By the way, some investors don't need debt service; they pay cash.

Cap Rate

I teach the capitalization rate to my managers and maintenance people so that they begin to understand value. Cap rate is expressed as a percentage. For example, a property with a $200,000 net operating income (NOI) and a cap rate of .06 equals a value of $3,333,000.

$200,000 NOI divided by .06 = $3.333 million

If the building manager can increase the NOI by $50,000 annually, that increases the value to $4.2 million, which is an 833 percent increase in value.

Concessions

You want to attract tenants, and one way to do that is to offer concessions, such as a month of free rent or paying for moving fees. In a strong market where occupancies are high, little or no concessions are offered. When occupancies are low, concessions are in play. It is a simple supply and demand issue.

REIT
Real Estate Investment Trusts are securities that sell like a stock on the major exchanges. The trust invests in real estate. There are special tax opportunities, and REITs may provide investors high yields and a simple way of getting involved in real estate.

Tenant Improvements or Tenant Improvement Allowance (TI)
Some tenants want to alter their space, and this will be part of the lease agreement. When you consider offices, you can imagine each business might want to customize to accommodate their best practices. The building owner is responsible for making these alterations. (These are used in commercial real estate, not in multifamily properties.)

Rentable Square Feet (RSF) vs. Usable Square Footage
Every rental space has usable square footage. Then, on each floor of a building, there are also

common areas. Combine the two, and you get rentable square footage. (These are used in commercial real estate, not in multifamily properties.)

Rent Escalations

Your leases will likely state periodic rate hikes that are meant to keep up with inflation. This is common practice in commercial real estate.

Renewal Rate

You need to know the renewal rate because it affects income and expenses.

For example, ten annual leases expire in any given month, and only five tenants renew. In this case, you have a 50 percent renewal rate. This is important to note because the tenants that move out will cost you maintenance expenses–in short, the cost of preparing for the next tenant—painting, cleaning, and repairs. Those that do renew will get a slight rent increase that brings in more revenue.

Full-Service Gross Leases (FSG)

This means the tenant pays one amount that covers everything—rent as well as all the management costs of the space, including utilities, repairs, and taxes.

Broker Opinion of Value (BOV)

A good real estate broker who is helping either the buyer or seller ought to be able to assess the value of a property. This helps determine an appropriate bid for purchase. Sometimes the broker will charge a fee for this.

Debt Service Coverage Ratio (DCR)

This is a key term because it reveals your ratio of available cash used for paying the debt service. This measures an entity's ability to produce enough cash to cover its debt, including principal and interest.

Modest Beginnings

There is no shame in beginning at the beginning. You can't learn it all in one afternoon. Most people I know who have succeeded in real estate are avid readers. They eat knowledge for breakfast, fully appreciating that you must start somewhere, and the learning never ends.

GLENNISM #7:
REAL ESTATE IS LIKE A SECOND LANGUAGE

When in Rome, it's nice to speak Italian and know how to place an order in a restaurant, right? "I'll take two 44-unit apartment complexes and several duplexes on the side. And bring me lots of sauce." Learning real estate lingo is like learning French or Spanish. Memorize the most common terms and be able to use them in complete sentences, as though you are in conversation. It is also powerful to apply the terms to a real-life situation. When talking with someone who owns real estate, ask a question using some of these terms, and don't be embarrassed if you are corrected. Humility is the true path to mastery.

NOTES AND THOUGHTS

_____

_____

_____

_____

_____

_____

_____

_____

———

EIGHT

PARTNERING PATTERNS

Mastering the art of developing partnerships is an off-shoot of my belief that real estate is a relationship business. You keep meeting people with the hope that you can one day assemble a terrific team of people, all of whom have their own specialty or strength.

Some people will naturally look to their closest relationships—family members—to build a portfolio. I don't recommend that. When the going gets tough, and you must make pragmatic decisions about expanding or ending a partnership, can you distance yourself from family? That can create a lot of personal pain and antagonism.

For example, when my partnership in Austin suddenly ended and led to a lawsuit, I was not facing my brother or sister in court. I could be objective, up to a point, about who was making claims about me. I am thankful that it all finally ended without damaging my business or mental health or reputation in the community.

But I must confess, even I have occasionally broken my own rules and with positive results.

I've told you about my first days in this business when I held a maintenance/management position. One thing I did not mention was going to my parents when a winning opportunity came my way.

My work managing a small apartment complex meant that I met a lot of people. I also attended church and was not shy about telling everyone about my new career because I was proud of it.

One day, a homeowner in the neighborhood where I worked came to me and said, "I know you're in real estate, and I need to sell my house. Would you like to buy it?"

The man, who attended my church, had built a new home, and that home was ready to move into, but for some reason, he had held off trying to sell his former home. By waiting so long to put it on the market, he was feeling the financial pinch and wanted to streamline the process. He didn't have time to do the whole sales thing and interview prospective buyers.

I knew this deal was worth the risk because I was so familiar with the neighborhood, with the going rate for rent, and what type of living spaces were attractive. Also, the owner would allow us to assume his mortgage so that we wouldn't need to get approval from a bank. (This simple type of transaction is no longer available, by the way.) So, I readily agreed to buy the single-family home.

By now, though, you probably can guess that I had that age-old obstacle: lack of money. So, I did what any hard-working college student might do. I went to my parents and asked if they would invest with me.

My mom, Billie, and my dad, Ralph, were interested and showed some savvy. Their first question was, "Can you rent it?"

"Yeah. We can rent it, and we can all make some money. But we need a $12,000 down payment."

Mom and Dad had savings, and they trusted me. So, they agreed to buy a half share and provided $6,000 in cash. Now all I had to do was come up with my half, which I didn't have. Yet the house was such a great way to break into real estate that I took a different approach to making the deal. It's called begging.

"Mom, Dad, I know we're 50/50 in this thing, but I don't have my $6,000 because I'm in college, and I'm poor. Can I borrow my half of the money from you?"

Parents are not made of money in most families. They couldn't risk a bigger chunk of their savings, so they suggested a path I hadn't thought of.

Another rule I now abide by is to stay away from credit cards. Only risk money you have in hand. Don't get yourself tied up in a loan that may be offered with an unattractive interest rate.

I confess, I broke that rule too. At the time, I was still new to the industry. And technically, it had not yet become a Glennism.

My parents allowed me to max out one of their credit cards for my half of the deal after I swore to the high heavens that I would not let them down. That's pressure, right? Do you now understand why I suggest avoiding family when seeking a partnership? It tends to add an extra layer of stress.

Fortunately, by managing the apartment complex, I knew that the rents were going up in that area, and, in fact, housing was a little hard to come by. The next hurdle was finding a reliable renter. But even that was smooth sailing because I was showing apartments nearly every day. When a couple declined to sign one of our leases, I told them I had a single-family home nearby that they might like.

As soon as the tenants moved in, all was well. The rent paid for our mortgage payment, taxes, and the monthly credit card bill. Positive cash flow is bliss. But we experienced a bump in the road 18 months later when the renters gave us shocking news. I immediately broke the news to my parents.

"The renters are moving out."

Mom panicked. "How are we going to make the mortgage payment, and who's going to make the credit card payment?"

Could we have found another tenant? Most likely, yes. But even a small dose of stress gave me another thought.

"Well, Mom, maybe it's a good time for us to sell."

By then, I had my realtor's license. That, too, is an example of being in the right place at the right time.

A friend at college, a former roommate, was older than me and had already graduated by the time I became an apartment manager. He went into the mortgage business and, one day, surprised me with an offer.

"Hey, Glenn, I've got this house that I need to sell, but I don't want to hire a realtor because it would cost me a chunk of money. Why don't you sell it for me?"

He had done the math. His expensive home meant that he'd have to pay the realtor a hefty fee on the sale. But where did I fit it?

"I don't have a license, Byron," I said.

"Right. I'll front the money for your course work and taking the test. It's a win-win. You'll earn your real estate license, and I'll save some money on the sale. What do you say?"

"Dude, that sounds great, but won't I have to join the MLS?" The multiple listing service database allows real estate brokers representing sellers to share information that may attract buyers.

"Yes. I'll cover the membership cost too."

Let the good times roll.

My realtor's license allowed me to offer the rental property my parents and I owned without incurring fees. I listed the single-family home and sold it quickly. The proceeds paid the credit card loan and returned my parents' initial cash investment. On top of that, we had a $40,000 profit, which we split 50/50.

We'd done well, and my parents did not spare their praise.

"Wow, Son, do you have another house to invest in?"

My experience with my parents was my first partnership in a way. We didn't immediately jump back in the market after our initial success, but eventually, we flipped a few more homes at a profit. I don't want to make this sound too easy. Remember, these deals happened nearly 30 years ago. Obviously, that first deal put us at risk. There will always be risk when entering the real estate arena. That's why it is so important to choose the right partners.

Partnership School 101

Many partnerships eventually fail because the people involved did not pre-qualify each other by talking through the what-ifs of good and bad scenarios. It's a common mistake. And I count myself among those who did not take to heart how important this process is–until it was too late.

I was reminded of this hard truth while I was coaching two students at the University of Texas. Both were enrolled in the entrepreneurship program and had decided to become business partners. They came to me for advice after listening to my guest lecture at the school. I began our sessions with a series of questions that probed how they would divide responsibilities. Then, I progressed to hypothetical scenarios and asked how each would handle the crisis.

These were thoughtful young men who sincerely believed that they could work together. But after being bombarded with questions, they realized a lot more planning was needed before they could begin.

The gratitude they expressed convinced me that while many of us enjoy the idea of partnering with other ambitious people, we often don't know what questions to ask so that a viable game plan can be created. For that reason, I believe many business men and women would be wise to find a mentor before they shake hands and call themselves partners.

Partnership structures can be defined in a variety of ways. A little research will provide definitions of limited partnerships, sole proprietor agreements, S corporations, C corporations, and limited liability companies. If deciding which is best for you seems daunting, don't despair. A CPA or business attorney will coach you through the language and definitions.

Before you get yourself into that situation, let's talk through some topics and issues partners must address early in their relationship.

Sharing a goal of acquiring half a billion dollars in

assets begs some questions. Do the partners agree on the steps they must take to achieve those holdings? How will you divide the labor needed to get there? Who will do what? If a detailed plan is not created, one partner or the other may feel that they are carrying most of the load. That's when tension begins to build.

I recommend that you make a list of scenarios after speaking with various real estate professionals who have seen it all. Then role-play how you would handle each situation with a potential partner. Not every challenge will be negative. For example, if a firm is making a lot of money, one partner may want to distribute that wealth to investors, whereas the other wants to save the money for the proverbial rainy day. That's not a crisis, but it could cause an argument.

Another common agitation results from hiring a new employee. One partner thinks she brings valuable skills, but the other is unhappy with her job performance and wants to terminate her contract. How do you resolve those differences? Who gets the final word? Define policy before those disputes threaten the partnership.

The final word may be distributed across a series of issues based on the strengths of each partner. Some businesspeople have human resource experience from previous jobs and, therefore, might handle employee health insurance and other benefits. Another partner might boast an accounting background that recommends authority in some areas of operations, such as supervising and reviewing tax returns, etc. Share the burden of making tough decisions.

Defining the workweek is another area that is often overlooked. If I plan to work five days a week, but my new partner sees herself in the office only once a week, some resentment may develop—unless there are good reasons for that arrangement, and they've been fully discussed.

A lot of relationships develop over time as the strengths and weaknesses of each partner become clear. Some growing pains can be avoided by learning as much about that equation before shaking hands on the deal.

This became apparent as I was mentoring a friend named Jerry, who, after a couple of years in a partnership, was seeing cracks in the structure. The company had grown to a size that demanded that the partners divide responsibilities. My friend had experience handling either operations and property management or acquisitions, so he let his partner choose. Unfortunately, the partner ran with acquisitions but often needed my friend's assistance. For example, he'd been deep into his own chores when the partner would ask, "Hey Jerry, I need you to review this acquisition. And do you mind getting on a call with this equity group because they want to hear from you?" Jerry didn't want to create tension, but he had to ask, "But why do they want to talk to me?" The partner replied that he was told he lacked experience, and therefore the lender and investors needed assurances from Jerry.

What just happened? Jerry learned that his partner could not carry the ball in acquisitions. Had he done his due diligence early in the relationship, this may not have come as a surprise. As a result, Jerry was working double duty and beginning to resent the arrangement.

Get as much clarity as possible when choosing your partners. When I asked my parents to get involved in a deal, I didn't have to do any digging for secrets. I knew who they were by how well they had treated me throughout my life. In a new relationship, it is essential to learn as much as possible about a prospective partner.

But how?

Ask for permission to contact people in the industry who have worked with that person in the past. Does this sound uncomfortable? At times, it is. Yet, consider what is at stake—perhaps years of your life and millions of dollars in assets. Early on, I did not do my homework in this way. I was a trusting and trustworthy person who learned many important lessons from the School of Hard Knocks.

The truth is, most disputes arise from pride, hurt feelings, and unrealistic expectations. It's not always about the violation of a partnership agreement or someone dropping the ball. Ego also plays a role in disagreements that you hope will not turn into a legal wrestling match. The

more you know about each other in the beginning, the
better chance you have of ending partnerships amicably.

Trading Places

My story reveals that partnerships come in all vari-
eties. As you know, I partnered with other investors to
buy my first properties. Yet, it was not until I had 30
years of experience that an established firm offered me a
partnership as part of a deal to join their team. It was an
important chance to further my goals and create wealth.
My hard-won knowledge was an asset.

Later, when I formed my own company, I could
count on my long-standing relationships to get me
started. Loan brokers suggested properties, and a friend
I'd met while working in the Seattle area was ready to
retire and sold me eight buildings.

Even with serendipity on my side, I lacked a couple
of things that would help me grow: a good credit score
and liquidity. It was only natural then to seek a partner
who could bring the resources of good credit and liquidity to our venture. Again, the first rule is to find a partner
who can help carry the load.

There are all types of reciprocal partnerships in the
world of business. A braniac might need a partner with
superior people skills. Or a natural-born organizer may
seek a visionary. A gender balance might also work. And
cultural considerations in our diversity-conscious world

could be extremely helpful: does your partner speak a second or third language?

When you are new to real estate, you look to people who can help move you forward and upward. Some generous veterans of the industry and some friends and neighbors provided a lot of support and opportunity for me after I committed to this career.

Then there comes a time when less experienced people will seek your help. That was the case for me when two brothers, Jason and Branson, approached me with the hope that I could help them close their first multi-family property deal.

At the time, they were partners, and they were in the business of flipping single-family homes. Although that had gone well for them for years, they were aware that multifamily properties provided better tax breaks and profitability.

When they approached me, they had bid on a 184-unit deal in Fort Worth and put up some earnest money, and their offer was accepted. To their surprise, the bank declined their loan application and told the brothers they lacked commercial real estate experience. When they approached a crowdfunding organization for help, they were told the same thing.

There was, however, one way they might still seal the deal. Get a key principal (KP) involved. A KP has years of experience in the industry and has shown the ability to operate successfully in the industry. Even if banks like the deal—and they loved this one—they still must be concerned about who is handling the money and management of the property.

Rather than take no for an answer, the brothers contacted me and explained their predicament. "Would you consider partnering with us on this one deal as a key principal?"

My answer was the same as always: Let me look over your shoulder at the deal. If it is solid, then I'm in. If not, it might be wise for all of us to let it go. Again, I relied on what the numbers revealed, and I was impressed.

The crowdfunding investor and lender agreed to the deal after I agreed to sign on the loan, and this allowed the brothers to also sign as key principals, which added to their resume and would help them acquire future deals.

This was a partnership that came to me. I didn't have to go looking for it. My participation earned me a piece of the pie. And sometimes, just a nibble is immensely satisfying. You need not own the whole shebang for it to be advantageous.

Also, each partnership doesn't have to be an endurance test. Initially, we assumed this would be a one-and-done partnership, and that was satisfying because it involved more than just money. I'd helped these talented brothers overcome an obstacle, and we all moved forward in ways that were particular to our levels of experience.

The art and creativity of that deal were expressed in the way we shared knowledge, reputation, and a fine piece of property.

Our relationship didn't end once we took possession of the property. I remained a coach and was happy to answer questions about asset management. The more they learned, the better we would do when it came time to sell the building. As they progressed, we could also entertain other possibilities. At one point, I found myself saying, "Well, gosh, if you ever find other deals that are this solid, let's work together again." More opportunities are always welcome, right?

GLENNISM #8:

RISK ONLY WHAT YOU CAN AFFORD TO LOSE

You may be considering a partnership that promises big gains, and you're tempted to take a big risk. Be careful. If you wager only what you can afford to lose, a deal done badly is not the end of the world. The risk level is different for everyone. Maybe you have $10,000 or less, or perhaps you have $100,000 or even $1 million. Regardless, the rule still stands: Obey your tolerance for loss. There is another *ism* embedded in this risk/loss equation. It's about due diligence: know who you are partnering with by asking lots of questions.

NOTES AND THOUGHTS

_____

_____

_____

_____

_____

_____

_____

_____

NINE

———

THE IMPORTANCE OF RELATIONSHIPS

In the beginning, before you've purchased one property or taken a real estate course, you may feel small, like a cub who needs guidance from Papa Bear or Mama Bear. That's only natural when faced with an entirely new industry to learn. A teacher might encourage the beginner to be a grizzly or a lion or an eagle that soars. In other words, be brave and go for it.

But, come on, we've all seen those animated movies when a fragile creature slowly develops into a full-fledged hunter or leader. It usually happens after the cub has found a mentor. I highly recommend choosing someone who is willing to guide you.

In a sense, I'm your mentor for the duration of this book. I'm sharing knowledge with the hope that you'll understand that it doesn't matter where you start. What matters is where these lessons lead you. The road may appear long in the beginning, and yet you may be surprised how things work out once you take your initial steps.

My mentors have entered my life quite naturally. John Gibson, for example, became a key figure in my learning curve because I volunteered time working with the apartment association in my community. I was surrounded by generous people who had a passion for real estate and loved to share. Through the next decade and more, I took those lessons with me, even though John could not always be close, like Papa Bear.

Good things will happen when you commit to excellence. You'll choose mentors who will inspire you. By absorbing what they must teach, you'll perfect your skills. As you polish your expertise, you'll naturally become the big bear or lion or eagle. You'll unleash that power only after you've acquired the experience needed to be truly confident.

Sometimes mentors miraculously reappear in our lives. When that happens, you can't help but wonder if fate and the other intangibles of life are at play. But never forget, your hard work made miracles happen.

That's how I felt when I began my own company in Austin. To grow, I needed to acquire excellent properties that would attract investors. In an earlier chapter, I revealed how quickly things fell into place with the help of colleagues and business associates. One reason I did so well is that I experienced a windfall that I didn't see coming.

Back to the Future

The 44-unit Meeker House property in the Seattle area was my first taste of ownership. John Gibson had provided that opportunity, and the property eventually sold for a nice profit. But to make the deal, the mortgage was divided in two: The bank was the first-position lender, and I was in the second position because I'd agreed to carry back a note. This meant the buyer was required to make monthly payments to the bank and to me.

Unfortunately, the deal started to fail when the buyer had trouble paying the mortgage. If he defaulted, my partners and I would lose our profit. I had a couple of choices: I could let the bank foreclose and then take back the property, or I could pay off the bank loan and, in doing so, move into the first-position lender. But if I did the latter, I would have to come up with a stack of money, which I didn't have.

Fortunately, a colleague recommended me to a businessman who bought non-performing banknotes that were about to default. That's how I met Ed, who was much older than me and a lot wiser.

Ed understood my dilemma. He graciously played the role of Papa Bear by taking me through the process of negotiating a deal with the bank.

"Here's what you need to do," he said. "Notify the bank in the first position. Let them know you want to buy that note at a discount. I'll help negotiate those terms."

Really? The bank would accept a figure less than the loan they'd approved? Wow. That was big news for a rookie.

With Ed's advice and counsel, the bank provided a discount of at least 30 percent off the face value. As a result, the deal was salvaged, and my partners and I could keep most of our profit. Ed purchased a note at a discount from the bank.

What just happened? Ed became the new bank, and the borrower would be in default to him if the money was not paid back. Over time, the property's performance improved, the buyer refinanced the loan and was able to pay Ed at face value of the original note. But here is the important point. Although Ed bought the note at a discount, he was paid 100 percent of that note. I'll simplify the math. Ed bought the note for 70 cents on the dollar, but the sale gave him 100 cents on the dollar—and that's a nice 30 percent profit. On top of that, he was paid late fees. But there was one more windfall for Ed. The original bank loan came with a six percent interest rate. But Ed received default interest on that loan and received 18 percent.

Ed, who was in his seventh decade at the time, thanked me for the opportunity and remained a friend even as our business lives diverged. One day, ten years later, the phone rang in my Austin office, and I heard a familiar voice.

"Glenn, this is Ed. You always said that if I ever decided to retire, you'd be willing to buy my company. Are you still interested?"

"Retire? *You?*"

"*Semi*-retire," he said. "And you've always stayed in touch."

It was true. I had. And why not? Ed had become a wonderful friend, and I always learned something new during our conversations.

I was delighted to buy his eight terrific properties, though I was less enthused about taking on his management company. I had my own firm of that kind and didn't need another. Also, the price I would pay was more than it was worth. I mulled it over and then made an offer.

"Ed, I'll buy your management company if you agree to sell me your apartment complexes in the Dallas-Fort Worth area. How's that sound?"

"Gosh, if you're going to twist my arm. Who taught you to be such a tough negotiator?"

I laughed. "Tough? I'm a cub; you know that."

"You've come a long way, Glenn. And you've got a deal."

You might wonder, why would I agree to lose money on the management company? I sat back and took a wider or longer view of the transaction. By agreeing to the purchase, I'd gain access to eight apartment complexes that made millions of dollars in profits. My decision was a means to an end, otherwise known as a great opportunity. And remember, this came at a time when I badly needed to acquire excellent properties to attract investors so that I could grow my new business.

Being stubborn can be costly. Nobody wants to throw away money—unless more money is to be made. In short, I encountered an obstacle that I turned into a victory for both parties. Ed would be happy, and my investors would be thrilled.

In my early days, I might not have seen the big picture. It was mentors like Ed who, through the years, taught me to negotiate and find solutions that others might not notice such as, buying a non-performing note and turning it into a profit. That was not an area of business I would pursue, but I learned a lot from watching an expert in that playing field. Business is not just numbers or profits and losses. It also involves creativity, vision, and relationships.

None of the miracles in my life would have happened if I had not understood and embraced the power of relationships. I've learned from a pack of Papa Bears through the years, all with different sets of skills. Thankfully, after the mentoring phase, these teachers became trusted friends. Where would I be without them?

Case in point, buying Ed's properties was a huge windfall. It put our company on the map. When people in the industry learned that we just purchased eight apartment complexes in one market, everybody and their brother came out of the woodwork and wanted to do business with us. More opportunities came our way. We didn't have to search as hard for deals because we'd get phone calls asking if we'd like to buy a 600-unit or 300-unit complex.

At the same time, we marketed our achievements through press releases that could be distributed nationwide. Yes, we were tooting our own horn. From the highest mountain top, we shouted, "Hey, we just did a deal." Such news would not necessarily make for a story in the business pages of local newspapers. But within the real estate community, good news travels fast. Everyone is looking for a new pond to swim in.

The moral of the story is, don't be shy. Tell people what you're doing, even if you are at the beginning of your career. The squeaky wheel gets the oil because it makes a little noise. Avoid boasting, but don't think mere modesty will open doors.

The deals we made with Ed and others allowed us to grow $260 million in assets over a five-year span. By then, we owned 23 apartment complexes, and the huge growth meant our lenders, investors, lawyers, and brokers were all on a roll.

Expand Your Playing Field

Ed was in Seattle, but that didn't stop him from investing in Texas properties. The Lone Star State is a fantastic market, attracting businesspeople from California to the New York island. If you live in Wisconsin, you're not limited to buying and selling there.

Texas is attractive to investors because of its stable and diverse economy. Other states may experience huge ups and downs, but Texas, for the most part, traditionally has not experienced extreme cycles.

Compare that to a city like Seattle, which is affected by corporations like Boeing. When a company that size lays off employees, suddenly 10,000 people may need to pull up roots and seek employment elsewhere. Microsoft also has the power to swing the economy high or low. A surge of unemployment can create a huge surplus of single-family and multifamily homes. As a result, values drop, and your net worth takes a hit.

These same forces have played out in cities like Detroit, where the auto industry's growth or decline created an economic domino effect.

Meanwhile, in Texas, we've got more than one big player in the economy. Gas and oil may have their ups and downs, but then the military and other sectors of business also play a role, and even politics have an impact. The conservative leanings of the state shape tax laws and so forth. By comparison, despite our own troubles, Texas has been a fairly safe investment arena.

So, as you learn about real estate and where you might fit in, research the tax laws and other incentives in neighboring or distant states. Obviously, Texas is not the only place to buy and sell. Your decision about where to get started will be affected by your knowledge, family and friends, and other resources. Do you have access to subcontractors or relationships with attorneys or lending institutions? Doing your homework before making a move may save you money and effort. Know the advantages of where you're going to conduct your business, and take a keen look at the economics of that location.

Thankfully, the United States is a big place. Don't be afraid to look beyond the horizon.

GLENNISM #9:

FIND A MENTOR

Relationships will make you or break you. People do business with people they like, not with people they have to do business with. Don't be a jerk.

NOTES AND THOUGHTS

_____

_____

_____

_____

_____

_____

_____

_____

TEN

DREAMER OR DOER

Where can you find courage? Is there a school that teaches it or a store that sells it in a bottle or a can? Can you earn it in the same way you earn respect from others—through your behavior and good habits?

No. Courage appears in all of us only when we make positive changes in our lives, or step forward to take responsibility or show leadership in a family or group setting. I wish I could include a courage page in this book and encourage you to tear it out and put it into your wallet, then carry it everywhere you go.

But that's not how it works. Courage may surface at unexpected times or fail to appear when most needed. And yet, we can see courage everywhere–mostly, in the lives of the men and women you admire because they define the difference between dreaming and doing.

In high school, I wanted to be a cross-country runner. As a sophomore, I was barely fast enough to make the freshman-sophomore team. By the end of that season, I was unhappy with my performance. My coach could see my frustration and took me aside for a little encouragement.

"Glenn, you have potential. If you work at this, you could be a good or great runner," he said.

"But, coach, what do I have to do to get better?" I thought I had worked hard all season, yet that was not enough to yield satisfying results.

"Glenn, to reach your potential, during the off-season, you must run every single day," he replied.

It was a simple but powerful challenge. I realized I had started the previous season unprepared. I wasn't in shape. It probably took me the whole time we were competing to condition my body to be truly valuable to my team. Cross-country is demanding. It's not a sprint. You can't win the long race only with a big heart.

I took my coach's advice. When school let out in June, I ran almost every day throughout that summer to be ready for the fall season. Remember, I had barely qualified for the freshman-sophomore squad, yet as a junior, I made the varsity team and became the number one varsity runner in our school. We went undefeated that season and won the district championship. My coach was astounded by the strides I took in 1985.

I've often thought of the encouragement he gave me. Despite my struggles as a rookie long-distance runner, he must have seen something in me that I had not seen in myself.

I wonder, though, how many times had he encouraged an athlete who listened but did not rise to the occasion? Coach's inspiring words would have been wasted if I had not found the discipline to get myself outside every day and put in the effort. I may have dreamed of cross-country glory that first season. The second season was a phenomenal success because I'd become a doer.

You now know the importance of seeking teachers and mentors. And then, once you've got some knowledge, finding partners is another way of upscaling your industriousness. Partners of all kinds extend your reach into the realm of real estate, and if you've sought them out, that certainly suggests you're making steps forward.

Even so, at every step of your career, you'll need to take the initiative to grow your business and fulfill your dream. Your teachers and partners can only do so much. Don't wait for someone else to tell you what is next. That's your job, though brainstorming and asking for insights never hurts. In the end, the people we admire have done their jobs when they inspire us. Then, the time comes for the student to "pull the trigger" and make it all happen.

How do you rate yourself? As you dream of creating wealth in real estate, are you also willing to become a doer?

The Doer Mindset

Sooner or later, you must close the textbook, walk out of the classroom, and put your knowledge to work in the real world. Don't expect a marching band to give you a brassy send-off, nor will the mayor hand you the key to the city. At first, the only one who will notice the change in you will be you. Record those feelings. Be honest about them. Courage does not necessarily mean you are supremely confident. Nor does it guarantee success. But never forget or underestimate the power of that moment when you step into the arena.

"Courage isn't having the strength to go on – it is going on when you don't have strength."

—Napoléon Bonaparte

Many men and women keep a diary or journal to record ideas and reminders. Then, there are those who only keep a ledger to mark credits and debits. I suggest you keep a bravery notebook. Give yourself credit for each step you take to become a doer and not just a dreamer.

On some days, the entry will be profound. "I made an offer on my first property." Over time, the modest entries will also combine to make you proud. Taking the first step out of the classroom seems so small. Then a thousand steps later, the doer realizes its significance.

At the end of each month, review your bravery notebook. Try not to be judgmental. By scrolling through your previous 30 days, you are merely looking for proof that you are for real–that you walk your talk.

Or, after reading your entries, a knot in your stomach causes anxiety. Write that down too. While taking steps forward, I'm not suggesting that you never feel fear. Some men and women are more afraid than others when making waves. You may be afraid to make a phone call about a property listing or meet with a maintenance man to learn more about the upkeep of a multifamily complex that has caught your eye. Just jot it down, while also marking the fact that you made the effort to be in the real world. Courage does not necessarily matter if you're never afraid, right? When you admit you are afraid but make that call anyway, that's courage.

The bravery notebook may seem trivial at first glance if you have not realized that courage is a habit that can be practiced and developed. Your jottings mark more than the events of the day. They measure your willingness to fulfill your dream in small increments of effort.

My hope is that several months of keeping track of your acts of courage will provide at least two important insights:

1. After acting, despite your fear, you did not come down with the flu or break a leg or suffer a skin rash. The effort didn't kill you, right?

2. After reviewing your bravery notebook, you begin to express compassion for the person— you—who is slowly but surely becoming a doer.

It may sound contradictory to bring up partners again. Yet who among us doesn't often feel better about their chances when a friend, family member, or business partner agrees to help carry the weight of a new responsibility? There is safety in numbers, and the reason is obvious: we inspire each other.

It is not unlike listening to a group of musicians who play especially well together. On the best nights, they raise the roof. That said, each musician is no longer holding back. Each knows that he or she must bring something to the performance. They must be brave in the expression of their instrument; otherwise, the inspiration from the other players is being wasted.

The bravery notebook should also reveal that heroism is overrated.

You'll never be Captain Marvel or Superman or Wonder Woman, starring in a superhero movie based on a comic book or graphic novel. Or at least I know I'm not able to fly through the sky or lift a 187-unit multifamily property in one hand. This is an important truth to remember: It is not heroic to succeed. To be truly fulfilled, you are not required to perform miracles or cure the curse of poverty or secure world peace. Courage was invented by mere mortals for the good folks in this world who realize that each dream bears a responsibility to change, to evolve, to leave old habits behind, and invent a new, better way of traveling from one day to the next. It's not heroic, but it takes guts to go from dreaming to doing.

So, somewhere in your bravery notebook, jot the quote below and re-read it at least once every month:

"You have power over your mind – not outside events. Realize this, and you will find strength."
—Marcus Aurelius

You'll also find strength by proving that your faith in your new ambitions will reap rewards that cannot be predicted or planned. So many times in my life, the right person appeared to steer me or bolster my emerging sense of doer-ship. Those associations would not have occurred if I had not been actively *doing* the dream I harbored within. While taking steps forward, be aware of who and what you attract. Proof of your faith is out there waiting to reward you.

On the other hand, there will be setbacks and times when you feel vanquished and don't know if you can go on. I told you about 2008 when Heidi and I lost just about everything we had worked for and were forced to find a different path. Your bravery notebook wants you to be honest about all things. Express how defeat reverberates in you and how it may dim your dream or affect your direction and determination.

People who are courageous do not always win every battle. Decades ago, my cross-country team enjoyed an undefeated season, but most winners in every sport or business arena rack up a lot of losses on their way to the winner's podium. *Progress, not perfection,* is a fine goal, even as you strive to be not just good, but great.

GLENNISM #10:
A DREAM INVITES US TO COMMIT

Commitment is the difference between dream-
ers and doers. But before committing yourself to
creating real estate wealth, review some of the
successes in your life. What kept you going when
the going got tough? We make commitments for
emotional reasons or sometimes out of despera-
tion when we know we need a new direction in life.
You're not in competition with anyone but yourself. Avoid self-defeat by defining why you want
to make this dream a reality and what it will take
emotionally to stay with your plan.

NOTES AND THOUGHTS

_____

_____

_____

_____

_____

_____

_____

_____

ELEVEN

COMMON SENSE RULES

Economic cycles will come and go, and they will have an impact on your real estate portfolio. They will teach you a lot, too, and they will challenge some of the standards we discussed in earlier chapters. To stay strong in a storm of financial change, do not forget the power of common sense.

Only One Captain

Early in my career, I learned one truth that has never changed or been challenged: Nobody will care more about your business objectives and assets than you. It's your baby. It's your dream. Don't think you can hand off the responsibility and still get the quality results you want and need. Delegate authority in modest portions and never be shy about asking questions and exerting oversight.

Does that sound like I'm asking you to micromanage every partner and goal? That's not my intention. We

MAINTENANCE MAN TO MILLIONAIRE

all need help to fulfill our goals. You will have to place your trust in your team, and yet they will continue to need guidance and assurance, and since you are the captain of your ship, you'll continue to be expected to make important decisions.

Buy Right

You cannot manage away troubles you've created by overpaying for a property. Don't think that poor financial decisions can be fixed later. A bad deal will bite you again and again. Always remember an adage that many real estate pros learned early in their careers:

You don't make profit on the sale of a property. You make profit on the buy.

If you buy it right, you have a better chance of success for you and your investors. This might mean that you lose out on some opportunities that look promising. So be it. Remember what I told you in previous chapters: Don't become emotionally attached to the deal. Crunch the numbers. Trust real data. The chance for a profit—not the guarantee—is based on how you buy the property. This is true of single-family and multifamily properties.

Boots and Eyes

Always have boots on the ground and eyes on the market you are most interested in. Visit neighborhoods and specific properties. Get a feel for the area. But since you can't be everywhere all the time, you'll expand your chances for great deals by always creating respectful relationships.

When I began my first business in Austin, various brokers, former colleagues, investors, and bankers were my boots and eyes. They had an enormous impact in those early days because they clued me in on opportunities I never could have known existed, and sometimes set up business meetings that led to lucrative deals.

Step Away From Your Laptop

I know this modern age suggests that anything can be accomplished if you have a laptop and Wi-Fi. But mark my words: You cannot manage your growing portfolio from behind a computer. A hands-on business approach does not mean your fingers must always be tapping a keyboard.

Rather, you must step away from technology and visit your properties to gather first-hand knowledge and updates. This can be incredibly valuable and fun. It is a good excuse to get out of the office, hobnob with people from all walks of life, and allow others to share their experience and insights.

Inspect What You Expect

Just because you have expectations of the people who provide services and have been charged with fulfilling your management plan, make no assumptions that all is well.

Periodic visits to your properties will either thrill or disappoint you. Your eyes will tell you whether maintenance is excellent or mediocre. And chats with your on-site people will determine if what they say is what they do.

Here is another way of expressing this common-sense rule:

Trust, but verify.

As an example, I know that a simple directive to keep breezeways and stairwells clean and tidy will have a big impact on curb appeal and tenants' and potential renters' perspectives. For that reason, I routinely visit properties with my asset manager, Mike Woodfield. An inspection is not an insult to employees and service providers. We own the property.

On one occasion, Mike and I asked a building manager if she had vacant apartments that were clean and ready to show new renters.

"Oh, yes," the manager said.

"Great. Let's go look."

The first apartment was chilly, even by Texas standards. The air conditioner was on full blast. Who pays the utilities on empty apartments? The owner. Mike and I looked at each other, both assuming our monthly bill would rise.

The manager was quick to say that this was not standard practice. "A worker probably forgot to turn it down. We don't normally keep them on."

That sounded reasonable, but when we visited two more apartments, we discovered the same problem.

Mike and I were told one thing, but our inspection revealed a different reality: Trust, but verify. It's the only way to know the truth.

As we continued our inspection, we found breeze-ways that were not clean, cobwebs in light fixtures, and a bees' nest above a door jamb. If you saw that while visiting a complex, would you want to rent the apartment?

I told the manager that she needed to raise the standards. Mike chimed in with an excellent idea.

"We'll come back in a week to take another look."

Message sent. Our return visit fulfilled our expectations.

Peel Back the Onion

When I asked a building manager for a closing ratio, I was told it was 50 percent. That meant that for every ten prospective tenants who visited the site, only five would sign a contract.

On the one hand, that sounds like a pretty good batting average. But should that be the end of the discussion? No.

"But where do the other five would-be tenants go?" I asked.

Obviously, they go to another apartment complex. But which of our competitors do they prefer? And what are their reasons for rejecting our apartments? In other words, do we have problems we can fix to improve the closing ratio?

Peeling back the onion is a powerful habit that can bring benefits to many areas of your life. It is essential when building a real estate portfolio.

In this example, Mike and I noticed that the grass had not been mowed. Again, this may seem trivial, and yet, it sends the wrong message to the tenants. If management doesn't care about these details, which improve a sense of community, why should renters care? All renters judge books by their covers.

The manager said it had only been two weeks since the previous mowing, and our landscaping provider had us on their schedule. But a closer look at invoices revealed that it had been three weeks since the last mowing.

"It must be an oversight," I was told.

That might be true, but when we peeled back the onion, we learned that our landscaper's previous invoice had not been paid, so they dropped us from their schedule.

"Why did we ignore their invoice?" I asked.

And Mike added, "We've worked with them for years. They do good work."

We soon learned that the accountant for this building was on vacation. Aha! Was it tragic? No. Thankfully, this was an easy mistake to fix. But we never would have known the truth if we had accepted a generality—it's an oversight—and not asked a series of uncomfortable questions.

You're the owner. You have the right to dig for complete answers about core issues.

Trends: Control What You Can

Heidi and I and millions of other consumers learned some tough lessons during the mortgage crisis of 2008/2009. The obvious truth was harsh: we could not control the entire economy.

But we could develop better personal habits and control our spending. We sold everything we could, mostly at a loss, balanced our books as best we could, created a budget, and promised each other we would embrace a new phase in our life, which eventually brought us financial stability.

Another lesson from the 2008/2009 crash was the importance of understanding trends. Although that event was unique, the washout was also a typical phase in a cyclical economic pattern that we should have taken into consideration. As you build your business, study, and look for curves in the road to your fortune. To begin, consider the four phases of multifamily real estate:

RECOVERY: This sounds like a funny place to

MAINTENANCE MAN TO MILLIONAIRE

begin because it begs a question: Recovery from what? It means recovery from a major downturn that ended a cycle. Recovery begins despite the pessimism from those who have suffered a fall. This is the classic example of buying low so that you can sell high. After 2008, many wise and liquid investors began buying real estate at bargain-basement prices.

EXPANSION: Hungry investors gobble up real estate inventory. Why? Occupancy rates have improved, and the job market improves as new multifamily projects begin. Remember, the recovery phase must include expansion, or the trend will fall flat.

TOO MUCH SUPPLY: Then, we come to that phase where the rental market becomes bloated. Construction has created too many units, which means the occupancy rate drops, and the opportunity to raise rents cools. This is a good time to watch the "absorption rates," which are an important indicator for where we are in the cycle.

HELLO RECESSION: When there is a market glut, demand cools off. Why? Renters have many choices, and multifamily real estate owners may have to lower rents to win tenants in a bloated market. Also, in this trend, some construction projects are halted midway as money dries up.

The four phases of multifamily real estate will not play out like a football game, where all four quarters are allotted the same number of minutes. One phase may stretch out for a long time, giving the impression that nothing will ever change. But then, things do change.

Since you know cycles will occur, the way to stay afloat is to diversify your portfolio. For some investors, this might mean holding properties that are considered luxurious as well as buying in submarkets. The terms you've accepted for buying or selling a property might also help you stay balanced.

Again, diversification goes back to the idea of control or lack of control. Perhaps a new trend emerges in your local community when a major employer lays off a thousand workers. Could you control that? No. Nor can you control the weather or predict the turbulence that world events may create in the stock market. So, you do your best to distribute investments across a spectrum of properties.

You can learn a lot about economic cycles and how they may impact your business by reading various publications, such as those provided by Marcus & Millichap, CBRE, Colliers, and several other large brokerage firms that provide a lot of information about occupancy trends for multifamily properties. As the saying goes, knowledge is power. The more you learn, the better you'll be prepared for the inevitable surprises that demand adjustments and sometimes new directions.

Location, Location, Size

It continues to fascinate me that some metropolitan areas or regions may be red hot, while others may be struggling. This accounts for the skyrocketing cost of multifamily properties in San Francisco, New York City, and Los Angeles, which are priced higher than the median price across this nation. This provides another idea about diversification. I love doing business in Texas, but that doesn't mean I won't cross state lines for the right kind of deal, even if I avoid the Golden Gate City.

The size of multifamily buildings may also impact the economy and your portfolio. CoreLogic.com reported that in 2018, about 25 percent of all sold properties had only 20 apartments or less, while another 25 percent of sold properties had more than 300 units. When you then consider the location of these buildings, you begin to see why there is a wide range of sale prices. Small complexes in high-end neighborhoods will likely fetch a better price than that same type of property in the B-market. In 2018, a quarter of properties sold for $5 million or less, while an additional quarter changed hands in the $50 million stratosphere.

In the end, all this adds up to a lot of opportunities, no matter where you live and work. Never be afraid of the data because it can save you from headaches and financial traumas. If one set of numbers doesn't please you, keep looking; keep expanding your horizons. As the saying goes, it does not matter where you begin—but you must begin to reap the rewards of your courage and hard work.

GLENNISM #11:
MINDFUL VIGILANCE

When managers collect the rent at a multifamily complex, the money is not theirs; it is yours. Who cares most about how that money comes and goes? You, the owner. Vigilance is essential in all aspects of your quest to go from maintenance man/woman to millionaire. But it does not mean you must be paranoid or distrustful. Your attention to detail is a friendly reminder to you and your team that you are a mindful, caring captain. And your leadership ensures prosperity for all involved.

NOTES AND THOUGHTS

_____

_____

_____

_____

_____

_____

_____

TWELVE

EXPERT LEARNER

Luis was the maintenance supervisor for a 200-unit property in Austin. I don't recall hiring him, but he quickly became indispensable. He often came to me with good ideas for improving the performance of the building. He had an eye for renovations that would make tenants happy and allow us to raise rents. He also had effective suggestions for reducing operational costs by getting rid of tasks that weren't necessary. As you now know, these types of innovations are an important part of competing with other apartment buildings in the neighborhood while pleasing investors.

"That's a great idea, Luis." I said it so often that I finally had to invite him to have lunch with me so that we could chat. He wasn't just cleaning the building and seeing to those types of chores. He was thinking like an owner and manager. That's a rare quality for a maintenance man or woman.

I'll also admit that I saw a little of myself in Luis. He was only about 30 years old. He was married with a child. And he was industrious. All good things. In fairness to him, there was one thing he had that I lacked: he was good at maintenance.

After ordering our food, I said, "You know, Luis, you're thinking like a manager.

Have you ever considered going into management and taking an office job?"

"But, Glenn, all I know is maintenance."

"I disagree. All these great ideas you bring to me prove that you have the aptitude for a property manager."

It was news to him. "Really? What do you mean?"

"The way you process ideas about generating revenue and raising rents while cutting costs—that's the manager's job."

"Oh. Sorry. I just assumed it was my responsibility," he said.

"Don't apologize. I love it. I'm saying you don't have to stay in maintenance—not with your talent."

Luis was like a lot of people with natural skills. They take it for granted, not realizing they are unique. Not only did Luis handle the maintenance plan we'd developed, but he was great with all kinds of people—the maintenance techs, grounds crews, and the porters and subcontractors who would visit the building to make renovations. Also, his relationships with the venders who supplied materials and services were terrific, and that alone made him deserving of a raise.

I finally blurted out, "Dude, I really think you could be a manager. And to prove it, I'm going to promote you."

In the manager's position, he would enjoy a small raise in pay, and I promised to take him under my wing and teach him how to use the software we used to create budgets. I would also explain how to analyze our marketing and advertising plans, the kinds of tasks the property manager would normally take charge of.

Luis was a quick learner. He absorbed all the new knowledge and did exceptionally well in his new position. In fact, thanks to his smarts, the property under his direction came out of a negative cash flow trend into positive territory. All the investors who thought they might lose their money were thrilled with the turnaround. Luis had created lemonade out of a great big lemon.

Despite his success, Luis seemed unhappy. After prodding him with friendly questions, he confessed that he had a second job. He had been moonlighting at a big box retail store. He needed the extra money to support his family and pay for the sports leagues his son was eager to join. But by working weekends, he wasn't spending enough time with his wife and son.

"I feel like I'm a bad dad," he told me.

Another lunch together allowed me to learn more

about his cash flow needs. We discussed finance and spending habits, and I realized he was relatively frugal. We analyzed what he was making in his weekend job, and then I offered him a solution.

"Luis, I suggest you quit your other job and just focus on your work with me."

"But, Glenn, I already told you I can't afford that."

"You can afford it if I raise your pay by the same amount that you're making on weekends, right?"

He was stunned. "Why would you do that?"

I said, "Because I see great things in you, Luis. And if you focus on this one job and not spread yourself too thin, you could achieve great things for you and your family. You know me. I'm always saying, don't just be good, be great!"

Luis began to cry. It was not the first time I was the cause of tears.

"I've never met anybody that would do something like this for me. I still don't know why you're doing it," he said.

He may not have understood that the change was good for both of us. But he agreed to my plan and dedicated himself to mastering property management. He was exceptional because of his leadership, friendly manner, and knowledge of maintenance. If you are a maintenance man or woman and want to move up in the real estate industry, never undervalue the talents you already have. Those talents give you a unique way to contribute to whatever projects you're working on.

Eventually, Luis was so effective as a property manager that he got a better job with another company and began making a lot more money than he had with me. Now, he oversees a group of contractors for various retail malls and continues to manage properties.

Was I disappointed that he'd moved on? No, because I'd also taken the next step by creating my own company. And he helped me as much as I helped him—maybe more: Improving the cash flow of a property can bring millions of dollars to investors. And happy investors are always willing to take my phone calls.

These days, when we speak, Luis says, "Hey, Glenn, guess what? I got another raise." Or "Hey, Glenn, guess what? They gave me more responsibilities!" But it is not only about career. He also tells me about his son and the happiness his work has brought his family. He confides in me because he believes I'm the one who elevated him to his fullest potential. I didn't. The greatness was always in Luis. He was always that guy. He just didn't know it.

I believe there are many talented people out there who have yet to be discovered. They need somebody to recognize their basic gifts so that they can see them too. Many people lack self-confidence. They don't give themselves credit for their skills.

Does that sound like you? If so, maybe you fear that

self-confidence will make you appear arrogant. No worries. To get noticed, just make one personal commitment: Be great, not just good, at whatever you do. Just that shift in mindset will lead to more achievements than you ever thought possible.

Motivation

There is no magic formula for success. But there is a core value that most everyone who exceeds shares: motivation. They want to do the work and contribute to their profession.

I rise every day and pinch myself as I get into my car and drive to work. I know I'll likely have some challenges, and that's okay because I spend my days doing exactly what I want to do. I live and breathe real estate.

As you now know, my entry into this business was a bit by accident. I took a maintenance job to pay for college and found my calling. I earned my academic degree only to realize that hospital administration bored me, whereas real estate quickened my heartbeat. Fortunately, I had enough self-knowledge to realize that to succeed, we all must follow our instincts.

Motivation isn't a bunch of rules or a boss lighting a fire under you or pushing you in a direction you may not want to go. Motivation is spending your time doing what you love to do. Every profession will take dedication and resilience. Yet without the sheer enjoyment of it all, what have you got? A job you don't like much.

Don't take my word for it. How many times have you talked with a friend or colleague and heard them complain about their unfulfilling career? How many of them have a secret? They wish they had gone into education or engineering or music or any number of professions—but not the one where they've labored for 20 years.

Perhaps I was fortunate in the sense that I kept meeting good people who were willing to help me along the way. On the other hand, if I'm objective, I know they wanted to help because they could see my enthusiasm and natural gifts. Perhaps they saw in me what I saw in Luis.

Even with opportunities, however, we must be motivated to do more than learn. The learning opens a door, and then we must be willing to walk through the threshold into a new world that will be challenging and, at first, a bit overwhelming. Some people refer to it as taking a leap. Whatever you call it, if you're not willing to step out of your comfort zone or change your situation, slowly, inch by inch, you may not get what you truly want in life.

During a discussion about motivation, Heidi once asked me, "What was driving you?" My answer was simple. Deep down in my heart, I'd always known that I wanted to be a businessman. I didn't know how or when it would happen, and in the earliest days, I probably didn't know what type of business I should pursue. But that hunger was there, that need to advance and be my own boss was always there.

My answer reminded me of the job I had with the Marriott Corporation while I was still in college. One day, I learned that the hotel had decided to upgrade its television sets in each guest room, even though the ones installed worked perfectly well.

As the transition took place, the old televisions were stacked in a storage area. When I heard management would sell each unit for $40, I had a vision. "Glenn, you can sell those TVs to your buddies and others for $80. They're a steal at that price."

I started doing the calculations. If I could buy 100 for $4,000, I could sell them for $8,000. Lordy, Lordy, with a $4,000 profit, I'd be a rich man.

But where was I going to get the money?

Are you smiling yet? I went to management and cut a deal. I would be responsible for selling 100 units, but only a dozen at a time. If I could sell those, I'd use the profit to buy more, and so on. My apartment living room, hallway, and bedroom were jammed with huge boxed TV sets. I told friends and neighbors about the deal, and they all told their friends and family. Everybody wanted a color television for a good price back in those days. Within 40 days, I had hit my goal.

Was I nervous in the beginning? Oh, yeah. But I

wasn't afraid. I'd learned the difference between nervousness and fear.

Here's the *Glennism* lurking between the lines: opportunity is everywhere.

But where will the motivation come from?

What is in you? To discover the answer, sit with yourself, and pray if that makes sense for you. In any case, get quiet and let the truth emerge. So-called "good" and "bad" memories will float through your mind. Sure, you'll have regrets and remember events that caused you pain. I bet you'll also recall moments when you felt your blood heat up. Maybe you already know the answer to the question: what motivates you?

Expert Advice

When I work with people like Luis and other maintenance men and women, my goal is to get them to realize their expertise or develop an expertise. I don't care if you're mopping floors or taking out the trash, do it with more efficiency and skill than anybody else. If you're an electrician, doctor, or a dentist, or a guy that operates heavy equipment, be an expert at your craft. If you can master one skill, you show the potential for mastering others. And tell people, "I'm an expert." You have no idea how far your expertise will take you.

I learned this while speaking at a real estate event. After my presentation, I went to dinner with a group.

Long before the bill arrived, a man approached and asked, "Mr. Gonzales, may I buy you and your friends' dinner?"

It is not every day that a stranger makes such a generous offer. He could see my surprise and so offered an explanation.

This man had heard me speak at other events and learned about my career. He'd been in the trades for many years but wanted more for himself. One day, he told himself that he wanted to follow a path like mine, and by the time we met, he was well on his way to achieving his goals.

He concluded his story by saying, "Glenn, it would be an honor to buy you dinner because you've taught me so much even though we've never met until now. You inspired me, and, basically, I decided I wanted to be *you*."

The comment thrilled me because it was exactly what I'd told myself when I met John Gibson, the man who helped me buy that first small apartment complex. *I want to be him.*

Also, this generous man proved the point I've been making to maintenance men and women for years: if I can do it, *you* can do it.

GLENNISM #12:
OPPORTUNITY CREATES WEALTH

Opportunities can appear in unlikely places and provide what is needed in the moment. Embrace them. Even if they are not real estate deals, they may provide valuable lessons. Also, by developing the habit of recognizing a good opportunity, you strengthen your confidence in your business skills. Wealth rarely happens overnight. By seizing the day, you are multiplying your chances of succeeding as you move from maintenance man or woman to millionaire.

NOTES AND THOUGHTS

_____

_____

_____

_____

_____

_____

_____

THE VALUE OF REPUTATION

BY AL SILVA

Sometimes, things go wrong in real estate. One of the worst times for a bad turn of luck is when you are just about to close a lucrative sale of a large multi-family property. As a commercial real estate broker, I've witnessed the fallout that can happen from an ill-timed surprise.

All that came to mind on an afternoon in 2018 when I answered my phone and heard the voice of Glenn Gonzales. I wasn't expecting trouble. But that's what I got.

"Al, I just learned that one of the chillers at the Westwood property has stopped working," he said.

"Oh, no."

"Yup."

This was potentially a nightmare scenario for Glenn, the seller of the profitable property, the buyer, and especially the residents: how would they endure the unforgiving Texas summer heat without central air conditioning?

"What should we do?" I asked.

Fix the chiller was the obvious and easiest solution. Call a serviceman ASAP.

"No," Glenn said. "It's done. It can't be fixed. It needs to be replaced."

Bad news. This was not one of the AC units you jam into your apartment window. The replacement he needed had to chill the entire 187-unit complex and would cost $100,000. Somebody was going to have to pull that money out of their wallet or out of their hide.

While I listened to Glenn, I began to run through countless scenarios in my head. I knew from my experience that sudden emergencies like this did not bring out the best in people. Often, a last-minute Band-Aid™ would be applied to fix a problem that the seller might not even disclose to the buyer of the property.

Or, if the seller announced that a problem was discovered, an adversarial negotiation could flare up, and the haggling would basically boil down to who should be left holding the bag.

Even worse, many times, such an issue was enough to kill a good deal, leaving everyone involved bitter or disappointed.

The property was important to Glenn and me because it was included in a big portfolio of properties in the Dallas-Fort Worth area that he had purchased a few years earlier from Ed, one of my long-time clients. Glenn and I would go on to do many other transactions, but this huge acquisition had brought us together for the first time.

Ed, who was based in Bellevue, Washington, had asked that I broker the deal and meet with Glenn in Austin. When I arrived at the restaurant with my team, I was surprised to see that Glenn had not come alone. He too, had invited his entire entourage so that two groups of strangers could get to know each other and begin the bonding and transaction process. I was impressed. In time, I would learn that this was a classic Glenn Gonzales strategy. It wasn't enough just to do business. If possible, we should also become friends.

After lunch, we all caravanned to Glenn's offices, where we spent more time talking about the particulars of the deal. That's when we heard the story of how Glenn and Ed had become friends. When my group hit the road for the drive back to Dallas, Glenn's parting gift was a nice bottle of Cabernet Sauvignon.

My impression from our meeting was that Glenn had an ambitious plan for growing his presence in the D-FW multifamily airspace. But unlike many others I have met throughout my 15-year career, he was willing to go above and beyond the norm, and he valued relationships in a genuine way. I found him to be intelligent, warm, and authentic. There are plenty of smart investors out there, and many are good at raising money, analyzing deals, and even executing deals. However, the lost art of truly getting to know the people you are working with and articulating the win-win scenario that always results from those human relationships is what separates Glenn from others in our industry.

His appreciation for people in his organization, from top to bottom, is rooted in his humble beginnings. That moved me because I too come from humble beginnings, and I've promised myself never to forget that.

On the long road home, I realized that the Austin meeting was not only about Ed's portfolio. I sensed that I would be doing a lot of business with Glenn in the years ahead.

Fortunately, I was right, because as I spent more time with Glenn, I was very impressed with his way of doing business. Together, we analyzed and toured many properties, debated underwriting, and eventually determined the nuts and bolts of how we would approach opportunities together. Systems–efficient and humane systems– were an important part of Glenn's success.

We also spent a lot of time together at conferences and industry events, and this was where I observed that Glenn is one of the best networkers I'd ever encountered.

Whenever we crossed paths, he always seemed to be talking to someone new, and I found myself being asked by others at these events whether I knew Glenn Gonzales.

I've worked with a lot of players in the industry, and most everyone networks at conferences. But Glenn's ability to make a positive impression, find areas of potential cooperation, and then follow up on those encounters creates an environment ripe for new partnerships and new opportunities. That's the "secret sauce" I've observed in my dealings with Glenn.

Through the years, I not only helped Glenn sell property, but I also had more opportunities to work with him as a buyer of multifamily assets. The experiences were positive because Glenn always does what he promises to do, and he is always prepared and professional from contract negotiation to closing.

Also, his vast experience in property maintenance and management, initially as the "foot soldier" for other people's firms, taught him to see things others don't see and to recognize opportunities where many others miss out.

One example was his purchase of the 184-unit Village Creek Townhomes in Fort Worth. Before we agreed on a deal, I'd conducted 25 property tours for other buyers. Yet not one of them even toyed with the decision Glenn made after seeing the complex—he would add a swimming pool and community center.

Many owners in the B and C class multifamily airspace

consider pools a necessary evil, or they are inclined to remove the ones that already exist. Maintenance of a pool can be expensive, and they come with liabilities and headaches.

Glenn, on the other hand, saw an underserved tenancy that the prior owners had neglected. The missing link was a sense of community. By adding amenities, the apartment complex became more than just a place to live. Over time, residents developed a strong community as their quality of life improved.

Meanwhile, the value of the property also dramatically increased. That's a win-win in my book and another classic Glenn Gonzales move.

But what do all these memories have to do with the Westwood property and that busted $100,000 double-pipe chiller system that probably had not been replaced since the 1960s?

While I listened to Glenn talk about his options, I was lost in space, a captive of a wargaming spell wherein I considered every nasty scenario we might encounter. I felt it was my job to forecast inclement weather and then define a few strategies for surviving the onslaught. I should have known that it was a waste of time. I snapped out of my brainstorm when I heard Glenn's decision.

"Al, I'll tell you what. I'm going to order a brand-new chiller system and have it installed in time for property takeover at our closing."

"What?" I said. "Are you sure?"

"Yes. It's the best solution for everybody. Let's get it done."

There is a moral to this story. By doing such generous things, Glenn reveals that he truly cares about his residents, his employees, and everyone he does business with. He recognizes the unmistakable fact that by doing the right thing over many years, while working with many different people, a man gains a reputation. And the value of that rep far exceeds the cost of a chiller system, a swimming pool, or a summit-sized lunch meeting at a favorite Austin restaurant.

Such a man also gains lifelong business partners and will entertain many outstanding deals that other businesspeople will never get the chance to consider. He'll also receive the highest offers the market can bear on the assets he sells because he is known to be honest, humble, and honorable.

The story of Glenn Gonzales is a true story.

I am his witness.

Al Silva
Senior Managing Director Investments
Senior Director, National Multi Housing Group

Made in the USA
San Bernardino, CA
18 January 2020